From the files of the National Enquirer

Divinely DECADENT

LIZA MINNELLI

The drugs, the sex & the truth behind her bizarre marriage

BY SARAH GALLICK
WITH ̶ ̶ ̶ ̶ ̶ ̶ ̶ ̶ ̶

American Media Inc.

From the files of the National Enquirer:
Divinely Decadent — Liza Minnelli
The drugs, the sex & the truth behind her bizarre marriage

Copyright © 2003 AMI Books, Inc.

Cover design: Tony Ballester
Graphic design: Debbie Duckworth

ISBN: 1-885840-04-7

First printing: March 2003

Printed in the United States of America

10 9 8 7 6 5 4 3 2 1

A Hollywood queen gets married

Athousand friends sat talking quietly in the Marble Collegiate Church in Manhattan at 6 p.m. on Saturday, March 16, 2002. Many were Hollywood's richest and most famous stars, gathered to celebrate the wedding of one of their own — Liza Minnelli — who was tying the knot with producer David Gest. The ceremony was to have started at five, but Elizabeth Taylor had shown up without her shoes and the crowd waited while an assistant went back to her hotel to get them. Liza and David tended to last-minute details. It would be a spectacular show from a woman who had lived her entire life — the professional triumphs, the personal pain, the heartbreak and the joy — in the spotlight.

Liza Minnelli is second-generation showbiz "with a capital Z." Her mother, the legendary Judy Garland, adored by generations for her walk down the Yellow Brick Road, came out of vaudeville. Her father, Vincente Minnelli, later to become one of the most famous directors in Hollywood, was the scion of performers in a traveling tent show. Like thousands of Americans during the Great Depression, the two had migrated west to California, where they'd landed jobs in the "dream factory," as Metro-Goldwyn-Mayer was called. They met on the factory floor.

Possibly Judy Garland and Vincente Minnelli's greatest production came with the birth of their daughter, Liza. Liza has become an international superstar as a singer, dancer and actress, inheriting colossal talent and unrivaled energy. When she was 23 years old, Charles Aznavour introduced her to the French as "the American Piaf." When Mikhail Baryshnikov wanted a dancing partner for his first television special, he chose Liza. Bob Fosse cast her in the film "Cabaret," which became her greatest hit and won her an Academy Award. Her lovers have been some of the most brilliant and charismatic men of her generation.

But Vincente and Judy left their daughter another legacy — one of long-standing tragedy and hidden demons. Friends and fans alike watched as the vivacious, tireless performer they loved was replaced by a depressed, bloated invalid, unable to sing, unable to dance, barely able to move. She was in and out of rehab, on what's become the celebrity tour, with stops at the Betty Ford Center, Hazelden and Smithers.

By the beginning of 2000, even her closest friends believed that Liza would never sing in public again. And then, just like in the brightest movies, an unlikely

Prince Charming, David Gest, stepped forward and said, "I believe in you. You can do it." And so it was a slim, sober, revived and radiant bride who would walk down the aisle of the Marble Collegiate Church. No wonder the church suddenly resounded in thunderous applause.

Liza Minnelli is, finally, a woman who has loved and lost and lived to love again.

Like a true daughter of the dream merchants, she has delivered what all her fans hope is not only a happy ending, but also a new beginning. Dreams, magic and the power of song and dance — these are the things that Liza understands.

In typical high fashion, the ceremony itself was a fantastic Hollywood act, another glittering scene in the life of Liza Minnelli. Her fourth walk down the aisle was a seven-figure extravaganza of stars, schmaltz and surprises.

The bash started Thursday night, when pals Ben Vereen and Nick Ashford tossed a bachelor party for Gest, 46, at Nanni's on East 46th Street. Three drag queens dressed as Liza entertained the first-time groom and his buddies. David proved he was a good sport by laughing it up with the Liza look-alikes and applauding with gusto when one of them belted out "Cabaret" and "New York, New York."

"He had a sense of humor about it," said Miss Understood, of Screaming Queen Media.

On Friday night, Liza met the 35-member wedding party at the church for the rehearsal. There, she instructed the 13 bridesmaids — among them actress Mia Farrow and songstress Petula Clark — to wear black. Trim was optional, but whatever they chose, the dress had to be long. Whether they wore a hat or not was their decision. During the rehearsal, Mia Farrow read a novel called "Abandonment." An usher directed vocalist Freda Payne to enter the church "stage right," through a special entrance for the huge wedding party.

Gossip columnist Liz Smith, always a great friend of Liza's, reported that the bride was running her wedding rehearsal like "General Patton with a touch of her director father, Vincente Minnelli." Yet the General didn't approve when an exuberant flower boy, Spencer Hoge, lobbed his petals like grenades and made explosion sounds. "A little less sound effects, kiddo!" she admonished.

Liza reminded her bridesmaids that the wedding was to start at 5 p.m. the next day. "This means you have to be there with everyone else by three, so we can all be together and line up properly," she told them. The church was locked to keep out curiosity seekers and the entire wedding party reconvened at Liza's uptown apartment for dinner.

While Liza supervised the rehearsal in the church, her beloved David was downtown in the ballroom of the Regent Wall Street hotel, only blocks from Ground Zero, working with 52 performers who would entertain guests at the wedding reception. It seemed as if in choosing to have their wedding at Marble Collegiate Church on lower Fifth Avenue, the joyful lovers were saying, "Start spreading the news," it was time to bring people back to lower Manhattan six months after the devastating events of September 11, 2001. New York, New York was back — and better than ever.

On Saturday, as the hour of the main event approached, Kevyn Aucoin put the finishing touches on Liza's makeup at her apartment. He would stand discreetly nearby during the ceremony to "pat her down throughout the evening," he said.

Also on the job was John Barrett of Bergdorf-Goodman, going for something minimalist with Liza's hair. "Rather than introduce a spike look," he explained, "I decided simpler, and let the eyes do the work."

Stretch limousines lined the streets outside the church as hundreds of guests arrived. Inside, many gasped at the sight of the altar, which floral designer Preston Bailey had turned into an enchanted forest, with weeping willow trees dripping white orchids. "It was way over the top," said one observer.

Guests had been asked to be inside the church half an hour early, but some were still streaming through metal detectors and occasionally surrendering unauthorized cameras to wand-waving guards as the clock hit 5 p.m., the time the ceremony was scheduled to begin. Among those who had wanted to take snapshots were Jane (Josephine the Plumber) Withers and Mrs. Bob (Rosemarie) Stack, who triggered alarms with her three-inch-wide diamond and sapphire bracelets. There were more jewels in the church than in the Tiffany's display case a few blocks north.

At 5:15 p.m., Michael Jackson stepped out of a limo wearing a beaded black suit and an enormous glittering brooch around his neck. He escorted Diana Ross, Altovise Davis (in long golden sable), and a frail-looking Elizabeth Taylor draped in black lace and wearing — of all things — house slippers! An assistant was dispatched to Ms. Taylor's hotel to retrieve her shoes. Nothing was going to happen until Ms. Taylor was fully dressed.

During the 50-minute wait, more than 900 guests, including Michael Douglas, Barbara Walters, Mickey Rooney (with wife number eight), Tony Bennett and Anthony Hopkins, admired the extravagant decorations and caught up with old friends. Anne Jeffreys and June Haver shared candy with Robert Wagner. Barbara Walters, stuck in Saudi Arabia, couldn't make it in time. Her co-stars, Joy Behar and Star Jones, represented "The View."

Among those not in attendance was Elton John. He was uptown, at the Sony Music Studios, taping a concert of his greatest hits. Between takes, he entertained the studio audience by playing the "Wedding March." He told the crowd, "I'm so glad I'm here, so I don't have to be at THAT wedding. If you want to get married, get married. I mean, I love publicity, but puh-lease!" Another star definitely not on the invitation list was 80-something Ruth Warrick. The venerable soap opera star was telling friends that the groom had proposed to her five years earlier but she turned him down because she was sure he was gay. Gest denies Warrick's claims, insisting he's 100% heterosexual.

"There's more plastic here than at Toys'R'Us!" quipped one guest, surveying the crowd. Other guests were a bizarre assortment ranging from 1960s sex kitten Carroll Baker to legends from TV's early days, like Gale Storm of "My Little Margie" and Anne Jeffreys of "Topper." Mickey Rooney had appeared with the bride's mother in the Andy Hardy series. Margaret O'Brien was a child star who had watched the romance blossom between Judy and Vincente on the set of "Meet Me in St. Louis" in 1944. Singers Tito Jackson and Michael McDonald of the Doobie Brothers had known the groom since they all played in the Encino Little League.

Everyone knew that Liza had met her husband-to-be at the Michael Jackson concert Gest produced last September, and it surprised no one that the groom was handling these nuptials like a Hollywood production. The perfectionist producer had supervised every detail of the ceremony. "David made incredible demands on the church," one guest confided, "making attendants move an organ and all the furniture off the altar."

Now David waited anxiously at that altar for his bride. His appearance — a hot topic even before the wedding — was enhanced by plucked eyebrows, lifts in his shoes and a generous application of facial bronzer. Watching him, some of the guests gossiped about his celebrated collection of Lalique crystal and Shirley Temple dolls in a shrine-like display in his apartment.

Everyone stood and looked to the rear of the church as the bridesmaids began to make their way down the center and side aisles carrying bouquets of red roses. ABC news correspondent Cynthia McFadden was in black-lace beaded Arnold Scaasi. Model/actress Marisa Berenson wore a backless black and white Gianfranco Ferre. The bridesmaids were followed by the flower children, two girls and two boys, including the exuberant Master Hoge, tossing rose petals the way Liza had taught him.

At 6:15 p.m., Natalie Cole stood at the center of the altar and sang "Unforgettable." At the climax, she beckoned to the back of the church: It was time for Liza to make her entrance. The orchestra began to play "Embraceable You," Vincente's favorite song.

The 56-year-old bride, who had dropped 90 pounds in the past year, entered on the arm of Bill LaVorgna, her longtime musical conductor. After years of health problems, she glowed in a low-cut, off-the-shoulder ivory sequined three-quarter-length gown designed by Bob Mackie. At the last minute she had decided against wearing the headdress, fretting that it would hide the beautiful diamond earrings her husband-to-be had given her or muss her hair. Michael Jackson fumbled with Liza's train until co-matron of honor Marisa Berenson took it off his hands.

Prepared to exchange vows, the couple stood before Rev. Arthur Caliandro. David whispered, "Liza, I love you more than words can say. You make me a complete person. You are everything to me. I cannot think of life without you."

Liza responded, "David, you don't have to live life without me. One day at a time, I belong to you. I honor you. I adore you."

David took his bride in his arms and kissed her passionately until Rev. Caliandro gently reminded them, "I'm not through yet."

The vows were next.

"I, David," the groom began, "take thee, Liza, to be my wedded wife, from this day forward, for better or for worse, for richer or poorer, in sickness and in health, to love and to cherish, till death do us part, in accordance with God's holy ordinance. Thereto I give you my love."

Liza gazed lovingly into David's eyes and repeated these words of everlasting love. After another passionate kiss with her husband, Liza broke into an impromptu tap dance, blowing kisses and bowing to their guests.

It was 6:30 p.m. when Shirley Cesar, the queen of gospel, sang "Amazing Grace," and Mrs. David Gest walked out of the church wrapped in a floor-length white mink coat, a gift from designer Dennis Basso. The coat covered Liza like a snowdrift down to the tips of her open-toed Manolo Blahniks. Out on the sidewalk, she tossed her white bouquet to the crowd.

She was already inside her white stretch limousine when, from behind a velvet rope, a fan shouted a question.

"Will it last?"

"It darn well better," Robert Goulet shouted back, "or I'll give her a spanking!"

"You must hand it to David Gest," said Cindy Adams. "He pulled off the grandest wedding since Charles and Diana." Co-best man Tito Jackson, who has known David since they were 12 years old, agreed. "It was a great thing to see two people so in love."

The caravan of limousines headed downtown to the Regent Wall Street hotel for Act Two of the Liza and David Show: the reception. Outside the hotel, bleachers had been set up for the fans, proving once again that no small detail gets by David Gest. Spotlights beamed in the sky as guests entered the hotel's grand ballroom under a white canopy.

Only Michael Jackson (and his bodyguards) slipped in through the building's rear entrance. Garlands of red and white flowers festooned every one of the ballroom's 60-foot marble columns. Lighting designer

Bentley Meeker had created a shining crescent moon and stars on the ceiling. Guests flashed their black invitations and were directed to assigned tables covered with red linen and thousands of burgundy, red and hot pink roses.

From the moment they entered the great hall, there was music, music, and more music. A 60-piece orchestra backed a steady stream of guest singers, from Little Anthony and the Imperials to the Doobie Brothers and Donny Osmond. Disco queen Gloria Gaynor belted out "I Will Survive."

The guests dined on shrimp and porcini-crusted beef. After Michael Jackson gave the only toast of the evening, Liza cut the 12-tier wedding cake made and decorated by Sylvia Weinstock in an art nouveau style. Six feet high, the cake was filled with chocolate cream.

"Everywhere you looked, there was a star," said one guest, noting the presence of best-selling author Dominick Dunne, Arlene Dahl, songbird Mya and builder Donald Trump. Joan Collins was seen leading her new husband, 36-year-old Percy Gibson, around like a puppy. Little Richard ducked into the ladies room as Rosie O'Donnell was heard pleading, "Will someone let up with the perfume! I can't breathe!" David Hasselhoff had nothing but good things to say about the bride, explaining, "The theme song I think of all the time is 'I'm Still Standing.' Liza just keeps coming back."

What a long, strange trip it's been for a Hollywood princess.

CHAPTER 1

Princess Liza May

**"My mother gave me my drive,
but my father gave me my dreams."**

Judy Garland and Vincente Minnelli fell in love on a movie set when Vincente directed Judy in "Meet Me in St. Louis" in 1944. A year later, on June 15, 1945, a week after Judy's first divorce (from composer David Rose) was final, and five days before the bride turned 22, they were married at the home of Judy's mother.

With his thick lips, receding chin and prominent nose, 42-year-old Vincente Minnelli was an unlikely husband for one of Hollywood's brightest young stars. Leading lady Kathryn Grayson claimed she couldn't bear to look at him. "He had this affliction," she explained. "He was totally unattractive." Vincente was extremely effeminate as well. In his early years in Hollywood, he showed up on movie sets wearing more makeup than a starlet. According to Judy

Garland's biographer, Gerald Clarke, "Vincente was indeed homosexual, or at least largely so."

But Judy knew what she wanted, and she stopped the gossip about her husband's sexual preferences — temporarily, at least — when she became pregnant immediately.

The night his wife went into labor, Vincente kept vigil at Cedars of Lebanon Hospital with Judy's great friend and sometime lover, Frank Sinatra.

Liza May Minnelli was born on March 12, 1946. Her adoring parents named her Liza for a Gershwin song they loved and May for Vincente's mother, but they affectionately called her Princess Liza. She was christened by an Episcopalian priest, and her godparents were Kay Thompson and her husband, radio producer Bill Spier.

Princess Liza was born into a world of brilliance, bisexuality and betrayal. Yet she has always stressed the happy times she had with her parents before they divorced when she was five. From the cradle on, she had a relentlessly sunny optimism that made people smitten with her.

Lucille Ball, who had just been directed by Vincente in "Ziegfeld Follies," was one of Liza's first fans. "I was in love with Liza before I had any children," she said. "Liza was my first love." When Lucy's only son, Desi Arnaz, Jr. was born 7 years later, Lucy could not have dreamed that her "first love" Liza would one day break the boy's heart.

A lot was going on in Liza's childhood home on Evanview Drive in the Hollywood Hills that would've tested her pluckiness, had she been old enough to be aware of it.

At the time, Judy was making the transition from the child star of "The Wizard of Oz" to adult roles in movies like "The Harvey Girls." But despite the fact that she had just renewed a contract at MGM that made her one of the highest paid stars in Hollywood, there were signs of trouble. Judy was bitterly estranged from her own mother, whom she blamed for pushing her into a career, and directors had been ordered to schedule filming around her volatile mood swings. Before Liza was born, her mother had tried to commit suicide three times.

One afternoon in the summer of 1947, when Liza was barely a year old, Judy arrived home early and surprised Vincente in bed with a man. Her reaction was to run to the bathroom, where she began hacking at her wrists with a razor until Vincente was able to wrestle it away. She returned to the studio the next day with bandages on her wrists.

He tried to protect her by keeping her breakdown out of the papers, but the infamous Hollywood rumor mill was spinning lurid tales of her drug abuse, especially her love of prescription pills. She had become notorious for stripping the medicine cabinet in the bathroom of any home she happened to visit. Judy's condition deteriorated. By the time her current movie, "The Pirate" (in which Vincente was directing her), finally wrapped, her latest psychiatrist recommended that she remove herself from her studio and home environments and she was sent to a Las Campanas clinic to recuperate.

Feeling helpless, Vincente tried to shelter Liza from the truth about her mother. "Mama went away for a little while," he told her, "but she'll be back soon."

It was weeks before Liza was brought down for a brief but emotional reunion with Mama, who was then shipped to the Austin Riggs clinic in Stockbridge, Calif.

"I can't stand it here," Judy reportedly told a doctor at Austin Riggs. "It's too quiet."

His response: "When you don't have a lot of noise around you, the noise inside you becomes overwhelming."

Judy was released from Austin Riggs in time to begin filming "The Easter Parade" with Gene Kelly, but she continued to see a parade of psychiatrists. So important was Judy's happiness to Vincente and MGM that when her latest psychiatrist suggested that Vincente be replaced as her director on "Easter Parade," he agreed. "You symbolize all her troubles with the studio," the psychiatrist told him. The next doctor suggested that Judy have somewhere to go whenever she felt the need to get away, so they bought a second house on Sunset Boulevard.

When Gene Kelly broke his leg, Fred Astaire was lured out of retirement to replace him in "Easter Parade." Astaire and Judy got along so beautifully that she talked about seducing him, but he turned out to be the rarest thing in Hollywood: a faithful husband. With no problems on the set and Judy feeling secure, they wrapped "Easter Parade" on schedule and $191,280 under budget. Released that summer, the movie became MGM's biggest hit of 1948, saving the studio from financial ruin.

MGM immediately moved to re-team Judy and Astaire in another musical, "The Barkleys of Broadway." It was obvious during rehearsals that Judy was too exhausted and sick to perform. Her nemesis, Dore Schary, the new head of production, sent her a registered letter informing her that she was dropped from "The Barkleys" and her salary suspended.

The ugly details about her mother's career and mental condition were concealed from little Liza. She has claimed that she mostly remembers only "that Mama went away." She has happy memories, too, of attending lavish birthday parties with playmates Mia Farrow and Candice Bergen. Television's Murphy Brown remembers that at these parties were "trained dog acts, magicians, cartoons, triple screenings of new movies — every imaginable extravagance. One of our friends even had an electric waterfall."

Liza remembers a picture flashing through her mind during one of these baby bacchanals. "I had a feeling this is not the average. This isn't the ordinary life."

Liza claims that as a child, she was never interested in watching Mama on the set. "After all, I could always see and hear her at home." But when Judy's director needed a toddler for the last scene of her latest musical, "In the Good Old Summertime," 2 1/2-year-old Liza made her movie debut.

"Summertime" opened at Radio City Music Hall in August 1949, but the skies were darkening again for Judy. She was supposed to start filming "Annie Get Your Gun," which had been a huge Broadway hit for Ethel Merman, and by April 1, she had recorded the entire score.

Then, her demons reappeared. As word about Judy Garland's notorious drug problems spread around town, the newly intolerant regime at MGM put her on suspension and replaced her with Betty Hutton.

Even 3 1/2-year-old Liza shunned her, recoiling at the stench of paraldehyde (a liquid used in medicine as a sedative) that surrounded her Mama. Gerald Clarke says that at one point a group of doctors were comparing notes on her case in a corner of her darkened bedroom. "Judy sat up and glared at them," Clarke writes. "There is something you fools do not understand. I am an addict. And when I want something, I can get it."

On May 29, 1949, Judy was sent to Peter Bent Brigham Hospital in Boston to try to pull herself together. This seemed promising, since unlike Las Campanas and Austen Riggs, Brigham was an ordinary hospital, not a psychiatric clinic, and Judy never believed her problems were mental.

Liza and Daddy accompanied Mama on the drive to the train station. When it was time for her mother to board, Liza later recalled, "She carried on so much that Daddy hopped on the train and went with her. I sobbed and screamed to be taken, too, but all I could do was stand there and watch the train pull away." Liza's nanny and chauffeur took her home. Three days later, Daddy came back, bringing her a drum he'd bought in Albuquerque. Liza beat her drum until it fell apart.

Judy returned home in early September 1949. MGM immediately put her into "Summer Stock" with a carefully selected cast and crew that was made up of people she had worked well with before, beginning with Gene Kelly. Yet pressure was immediately on her to lose weight. She went back on diet pills, and a slim and wired Judy returned to film the dance scene for the "Get Happy" finale, the number made "Summer Stock" a hit.

MGM rushed Judy into "Royal Wedding," teaming her again with Fred Astaire. The first-time director was 26-year-old Stanley Donen, who was best known as Gene Kelly's collaborator and assistant. Donen was under strict orders to keep Miss Garland on time.

Tension between Donen and the troubled star began during rehearsals, where he reprimanded several times for lateness. When he ordered a Saturday rehearsal, she called in sick with a migraine. Before sundown on June 19, 1950, she received at her home an official letter notifying her that she was under suspension once again.

Upon reading the letter, she ran to the bathroom screaming, "I want to die!" Locking herself inside, she smashed a drinking glass and proceeded to slash her own throat. Vincente finally broke down the door and, with family friend Carlton Alsop, rushed Judy to a doctor who bandaged her up and pronounced, luckily, her injuries were not serious. The story got out at once, setting off lurid headlines like the Los Angeles Mirror's "Judy Cuts Throat over Lost Job" and confirming her growing reputation as unstable, unmanageable and suicidal. Everyone involved knew that Judy was through at MGM, and probably in the industry. On September 29, 1950, the studio officially released Judy from her contract.

As Liza recalls, "After that . . . my father moved out, and that was the end of their marriage and our being together." Judy and Vincente announced they were separating the first week of December 1950.

Judy left Vincente and 4 1/2-year-old Liza behind and went to spend time in New York. She was

frequently seen on the nightclub circuit with a new
man, producer Sid Luft. In an eerie foreshadowing of
Liza's relationship with David Gest, Sid assured the
overweight, emotionally shattered Judy she still had a
future in the business. He believed that she was a
brilliant entertainer who needed only the right showcase.

Judy's divorce from Vincente became final on
March 22, 1951. They agreed to share custody of Liza
informally, which meant that a week later Judy left her
5-year-old girl with Vincente when she sailed to
England on the Ile de France. Sid joined her at the
Dorchester Hotel in London, and they prepared for an
opening at the Palladium April 9. It was one of the
greatest comebacks in show business. Judy performed
the songs from her films that fans loved — "You Made
Me Love You," "Get Happy," and, dressed as a hobo,
"A Couple of Swells." And of course she sang her
anthem, "Over the Rainbow."

Judy was pulling in $20,000 a week as the bright
new star of British vaudeville.

In Hollywood, Vincente brought Liza to the studio
almost every day. But little Liza was never interested
unless he was shooting a musical number or something
spirited. If he was filming a love scene, she would slip
out of her chair and run to another set until she could
find someone who was singing or dancing. She loved
to watch Fred Astaire when he was making "The Band
Wagon" and even then could mimic his dance steps.
Cyd Charisse was another favorite. Liza wanted to
grow up and be a dancer like her.

There is a poignant Life photo from the summer of
1950 of a gleeful little Liza rushing into the arms of
her mother after a six-month separation. In October,

Judy brought her act to the Palace Theater in New York. The review accompanying the photo raved, "The girl with the voice meant equally for lullabies, love songs and plain whooping and hollering deserved the most overworked word in her profession: great." The following spring, Judy opened at the Los Angeles Philharmonic Auditorium, played there for a month, and then took the show to San Francisco.

One night at the time, Liza was watching her mother as she sat at her vanity table, applying makeup to go out. Mama asked 6-year-old Liza if she would mind if she married Uncle Sid.

Puzzled, Liza asked, "What for? Why would you want to do that?"

"Because," Judy replied, "if I do, then you could have a baby brother or sister."

Liza thought that made sense and gave her permission.

Actually, Judy was already pregnant when she asked Liza that question. Not long afterward, while watching the TV news, Liza and her father learned that Judy Garland and Sid Luft had been married in a small town outside San Francisco. Even then, Liza understood that "it wasn't my business when Mama got married, really, or to whom." She was soon calling Uncle Sid "Pop."

Her new baby sister, Lorna Luft, arrived Nov. 21, 1952, and it wasn't long before Liza was running the household. "One night Mama had a terrible fight with Lorna's nurse," Liza recalled. "Then Mama had to go out, and right after she left, the nurse packed up and left, too." Liza was barely 7 years old and didn't have a clue what to do with a howling baby. "Finally, I roused the cook and she and I coped until my mother came home."

Despite the struggles, Liza remains relentlessly upbeat about those years, especially when she was living in the same town as her father. "Throughout all the pressures, I could always get in a cab, and come and say to Daddy, 'I don't understand,' and have it explained to me."

Still, stability would never be in Liza's vocabulary. Eventually she would live in eight houses in Beverly Hills and three in London. Usually they moved in the night, one step ahead of landlords, irate promoters and angry hotel clerks. But no matter how broke they were, they always lived like millionaires and with laughter.

"Every time we moved I'd find myself in a different school," Liza says. "Private if we could afford it, public if we couldn't." All told, she went to 20 schools here and abroad. Often she was in boarding school and didn't see much of either Vincente or Judy. Sometimes she would hear rumors that Mama was "sick," but Judy always insisted that the newspapers "got it wrong."

By the time Judy closed at the Palace in February 1952, she had broken all box office records. Sid Luft had fulfilled one of Judy's dreams: He had proven that she was still a star. Now they headed back to Hollywood, a sweet three-picture deal with Warner Brothers in hand. The first film on their schedule was "A Star Is Born."

Vincente was happy to have his 6-year-old daughter back, and Liza would ride with him to and from the studio, spending the entire day by his side. After dinner, he would put her in a car and send her home to her mother.

"My father did his best to give me a normal upbringing. He really did," Liza insists today. "He'd ask me 'What do you want to be, Liza,' And I'd say, 'A Spanish dancer.' And he would go out and buy crepe paper from a drugstore and wrap it round me and he would then stretch it and put safety pins in and I would have a train and ruffles and he'd say, 'What does a Spanish dancer do?' and I'd say, 'Dance!' And he'd say, 'Then dance, Liza, dance!' And he'd watch me for hours."

But soon Liza would no longer have Vincente to herself. He had been introduced to 22-year-old Georgette Martel, sister and chaperone of Christiane Martel, then Miss Universe. A lifelong lover of all things French, Vincente courted Georgette while he was directing "Brigadoon." They married February 16, 1954.

In April 1955, Georgette gave birth to Vincente's second daughter, Christiane Nina, known as Tina Nina. While Vincente was at the studio all day filming "Gigi," Liza treated Tina Nina like her own little doll, dressing her in costumes. But an escalating conflict between Liza and Georgette only ended when the Minnellis separated October 13, 1957, and divorced in May 1958. Liza had Daddy to herself again, and for years, many of her close associates did not even realize that she had another sister, who would ultimately be raised in Mexico.

After school, Liza ran to MGM to watch the shooting the way another child might hang around her father's store. "It seemed like a factory to me," she said. "I loved it. I got so that I knew every inch of it, all the shortcuts to different stages and all the underground passages. All the people there knew me."

What really interested Liza was Rehearsal Hall B or C, where her idols Cyd Charisse, Fred Astaire and Gene Kelly worked. She would learn their dance numbers, then go home and practice for hours in front of the mirror.

Judy and Sid were so convinced that Judy would make at least two more films at Warner that after "A Star Is Born" wrapped in July 1954, they bought a mansion on South Mapleton Drive in Holmby Hills, where they threw lavish parties for Humphrey Bogart, Lauren Bacall and other friends. Judy invited a newcomer named Marilyn Monroe, and Liza was the only one who talked to her.

"She used to tell me how lonely she was," Liza said in 1972. "I told her that she had to talk to people and let them know she didn't want anything from them."

"A Star Is Born" opened October 11 in New York and was greeted with critical raves. Judy was nominated for an Academy Award for best actress. She was also pregnant again, and on the morning of March 29, 1955, Oscar day, she gave birth to Liza's little brother, Joseph Wiley Luft, always to be known as Joey.

Everyone in town believed Judy would win the Oscar that night. NBC-TV, which was broadcasting the ceremony, even set up cameras outside her hospital window at Cedars of Lebanon Hospital, so they could catch her reaction to the great news. Unfortunately for Judy, the news that night really was news. In a shocking upset, the Academy Award for best actress in a leading role went to Grace Kelly for her performance in "The Country Girl." To make matters worse, "Star" barely covered production costs at the box office.

After the Academy Awards, Sid and Judy were broke again. With no movie likely in their immediate future, Sid started planning another comeback tour. On September 24, Judy made her television debut on CBS and drew 40 million viewers. The network immediately scheduled a second Judy Garland special, which aired April 8, 1956.

It was in the fall of 1956, when Liza was 10 years old, that her mother invited her onto the stage at the Palace Theater in New York. It was a return engagement for Judy, and one that would go down in show business history. Liza enthusiastically rushed up and danced her little heart out while Judy sang "Swanee." Liza heard those waves and waves of applause washing over them and was instantly hooked. Pop gave her a $5 bill for her performance, and she framed it.

After Judy's second TV special, she began feuding with CBS, and the network canceled her third show. After appearing to packed houses in Las Vegas, by the end of 1957, she was battling with audiences there and walked out.

As if that weren't enough, Judy was also fighting with Sid. Their screaming arguments were familiar all over town. When the drama became unbearable at home, Liza would put her hands over her ears.

Inevitably, the little girl learned that it wasn't always so easy to shut the noise out. By the time Liza was 13, she weighed 165 pounds and was "a real El Chubbo," she later recalled. She had discovered her first vice — food.

Still, little Liza fought the odds and found success.

One evening, Vincente brought Liza to a dinner

party at Lee Gershwin's. Producer Roger Edens, her mother's mentor at MGM, was at the piano, accompanying Gene Kelly and Frank Sinatra. Then Edens turned to Liza and asked her to sing with him. Until then, these men who had known Liza all her life had thought of her as just a gawky kid with big eyes like her father's. But now Kelly saw that magic. He was preparing a television special and he wanted to put Liza in the show. The two eventually decided to perform "For Me and My Gal" — the same number that Kelly had sung with her mother in the 1942 film of the same name.

Although Judy approved of her daughter's appearance on Gene Kelly's television show, she quickly took steps to get Liza out of the Hollywood scene. After a success at the Olympia Theater in Paris in 1960, Judy became convinced that her daughter should study the language and culture of France, and she sent her off to Neuilly with six other girls and a chaperone. Liza learned to speak French fluently and studied at the Sorbonne. "I stayed for exactly one term," she has said, "which was about as long as I spent at any of the 20 schools I attended."

Liza was boarding in the French Alps when Mama and Pop came to visit. They were sitting in a boat, just the three of them, when Mama asked Liza how she would like to live in London with her and Pop and Lorna and Joey.

"She wanted to leave all the unhappiness behind in America and live in the city she dearly loved," said Liza. "She was wonderfully funny and whimsical about it and she made me roar with laughter. I told her that I would love to live in London." Liza did not tell her mother that during her semester at the Sorbonne she had decided she wanted to go into show business. Shortly thereafter, Judy took Liza to see some Broadway shows. Watching "Bye Bye Birdie" and especially the dazzling performance of Chita Rivera convinced Liza that she wanted to become a Broadway dancer.

"It wasn't that tedious process I saw at Metro," she said in 1972. "I could see it happening before my eyes. The chorus of 'Bye Bye Birdie' fascinated me. It had kids in it, and a camaraderie that I recognized. It seemed like an answer to the kind of loneliness I felt. Just friends kidding around, with lots of laughter."

It was while attending Scarsdale High School that Liza appeared in their production of "The Diary of Anne Frank." A generous benefactor arranged for the drama group to take the show abroad to Israel, Athens and Rome during the summer of 1961. Before she left, Liza visited her father in Hollywood, and for the first time asked him for advice about her performance.

"Listen to the director," he said simply.

Soon enough, as always happened whenever Liza settled into a routine, Mama and Pop were discussing sending her to yet another school. This time, she made up her mind that she had to take a stand about going into show business. She wanted to go to New York City and be on the stage.

"I didn't want to start my career in Hollywood," she has said, "because I had seen too intimately what Hollywood stardom can do to someone."

Liza decided to tell Vincente first. That was the easy part. He was pleased and fully endorsed her plans. Armed with his approval, she braced herself for a major argument with Mama. To her shock, there was no scene. Instead, Judy was deadly calm as she told her, "OK, if that's what you really want to do, go ahead. You have my blessings. Just one thing — no more money from me, ever again."

Most of the time when Liza has told this story, she's portrayed everyone as calm and adult about her decision. But once, in a 1970 interview, she hinted at a slightly darker picture. "Mama went on a kick every now and then, where she used to kick me out of the house," Liza recalled. "Usually I'd stand outside the door and pretty soon she'd open it and we'd fall into each other's arms, crying and carrying on. But one day she did it and I took her up on it. I went to New York. I had my plane fare and $100 and I've never taken a penny since."

It doesn't really matter whether Liza's decision was greeted with calm approval by two divorced but loving parents or whether a mother given to rages kicked her out and a distant father consumed by his work just let her go. What matters is that Liza, from that point on, was on her own and self-supporting. She took the framed $5 bill that Pop had given her and the rest of the money she had saved, and left for New York City. She was 16 1/2 years old.

CHAPTER 2

And now, Miss Liza Minnelli!

"If I held my own with my mother,
I'm not gonna be afraid of anything."

In the Big Apple, Liza stayed with a series of family friends. Her studies included time at the High School for the Performing Arts, and at the Herbert Berghof Studio. Meanwhile, she went to every audition she heard about, trying to earn her way into a role.

Just before her 17th birthday, Liza got her big break: the third lead in a revival of "Best Foot Forward." Most of the cast were "Bye Bye Birdie" alumni, and she was thrilled to be working with genuine pros. "Best Foot Forward" opened on April 2, 1963. A proud Vincente was in the audience, delighted with what he saw. Judy was supposed to be there too, but she never showed, insisting that she had been told it was the next night. Later, Liza decided that her mother had deliberately stayed away so as not to overshadow her. Judy came the second night and told reporters how proud she was of Liza.

Liza was earning $34 a week and that year won Theater World's Daniel Blum Award for the most promising young actress of the season. She turned down a better offer to do "The Unsinkable Molly Brown" that summer to stay with "Best Foot Forward."

"No one's leaving the show," she insisted. "We're having too much fun."

But Liza did take time off from the show to fly to California for appearances on Judy's glitzy new TV series, "The Judy Garland Show," and when she did, people who bought tickets to "Best Foot Forward" wanted refunds and attendance suffered. Liza was becoming as big a draw as her mother.

And, like her mother's, Liza's relentless energy was embodied in a fragile constitution. The combination meant a lifetime of health woes as she regularly pushed herself to the point of collapse. That was the story that appeared in the newspapers Nov. 15, 1963, when 17-year-old Liza, who had been staying with Judy at a new home on South Rockingham Avenue while discussing some movie offers, was rushed to Cedars of Lebanon Hospital. Every tabloid reader in the country was familiar with Judy's collapses and hospitalizations. Now, they read about her daughter's.

Ignoring questions as to whether it was wise to do so, Liza signed a three-album contract with Capitol Records to begin recording in 1964. While looking for new material for her first album, she was introduced to the composer, John Kander, and lyricist, Fred Ebb, who had just begun working together. They played her songs from the Broadway show they were writing, "Flora, the Red Menace." It was an instant connection and the beginning of a lifelong relationship. Kander and Ebb would eventually write all Liza's trademark numbers: "New York, New York," "Maybe This Time," "Cabaret" and more. That year, Liza's single "You Are for Loving" was released and hit all national charts. With her very first Capitol album, "Liza! Liza!," she was established as a major recording artist.

Maybe it was all too much to soon. One morning in January 1964, she woke up so sick she couldn't get out of bed and called a doctor, who came to see her. Her temperature was soaring and her legs were limp. After three days of tests, it was determined that she had a kidney stone, leading to nearly a month in the hospital.

Liza was in touch with her mother mostly by telephone, but when she was released from the hospital, Judy insisted she come to California to rest. Liza explained that she was going on the road with the stage show "Carnival," saying that she had signed a contract and could not walk out. Judy was furious. She had seen her daughter desperately ill in November and now she was hospitalized again. Judy did not want Liza's health ruined the way she believed MGM had ruined hers.

Insisting that she would do everything in her power to stop her daughter, Judy called the newspapers and told them that she had forbidden Liza to appear in "Carnival." They battled it out for two weeks, but Liza stuck to her guns and did the show. It was the first time she openly defied Mama. One critic noted that Liza, "although performing against her famous mother's wishes — brings out the very best in Lilli."

Judy's own career and personal life were nearing collapse. She had split for the final time from Sid and they were battling for custody of Lorna and Joey. Her drinking and drug use were out of control. After running through a series of lovers, she had married Mark Herron, a handsome actor from California who accompanied Judy on her endless world tour.

They arrived in Australia in May, but by the time they hit Melbourne, she was in no condition to perform. The concert was a drunken debacle and Judy was booed by the crowd and castigated in the press. The couple fled to Hong Kong, where she tried to get Herron to join her in a suicide pact. He refused, and she overdosed on her own. She was in a coma when he rushed her to the hospital.

While Herron waited to learn if his wife was going to live, he couldn't bear to go back to their hotel because he knew reporters were onto the story. He hid out in the bar of the Hilton, where he was distracted from his troubles by the entertainment act of Chris and Peter Allen, two Australians who sang, played piano and kept the show moving with quick comic patter.

The next day, Herron went to the hospital to see Judy, now out of her coma. She asked him what he'd done during the night. He said, "As a matter of fact, I went out and saw this fabulous act." He did not mention that he and Peter had become lovers.

Judy was furious that Herron was out enjoying himself while she nearly died. According to Peter Allen, "she ripped out all the tubes, put on a scarf and went to the hotel to see us that night. She loved me.

She told me I reminded her of Fred Astaire, and I thought, 'What a rude thing to say.' "

Apparently Allen had never seen Astaire in any of his early musicals, recalling only his appearance in "On the Beach," a less than glamorous late-career performance.

As Judy's star started to short-circuit, she looked around for some way to generate interest in her flagging box-office appeal and fading voice. It must have taken a great deal of courage — or just plain desperation — to ask Liza to appear with her at her scheduled Palladium show in November.

Liza just kept saying, "Mom, I'll sit in the front row. Honest, I really don't have to be up there." But Judy kept at it. "I don't want to do it alone, please do it with me," she pleaded.

Liza still refused. After all, when Liza started her career, her mother had made her promise not to sing any of her songs. She had made her way without Judy's help, she was on the brink of a terrific career — everybody but her mother was telling her so — and she felt that at this point she owed Judy nothing.

But Judy was shrewd, especially about self-promotion, and she was wired to entertainment industry reporters and columnists around the world. She put out the word that her wonderful daughter would be performing with her Nov. 8, 1964. Liza was trapped.

Liza had never worked with her mother on a joint live concert. When Liza was small and jumped on stage to dance while Judy sang, it had been an unrehearsed and spontaneous thing. This would be different. Judy turned to Marvin Hamlisch for the musical arrangements and rehearsed like mad before she even arrived in London.

On the big night, midway through her first set, Judy made a dignified announcement to her audience: "And now, ladies and gentlemen, Miss Liza Minnelli." The applause was merely polite.

But at the end of Liza's first song, it was thunderous. "Hello, Dolly!" became "Hello, Liza! Hello, Mama!" They joined voices on "We Could Make Such Beautiful Music Together." And Liza sang a medley to her mother that wove together lines from "Take Me Along," If I Could be with You," "They Can't Take that away from Me" and "By Myself" and "Mammy." The two performed over 20 duets. Not everyone was fooled, however. A Times critic noted that "beneath the sentimental veneer, a strong and often cutting sense of challenge is evident."

"Nobody expected it," Peter Allen said in 1972, "and I watched to see how Judy would react and it was weird. Love-hate. She was as startled as anybody, and proud, but she's never had to share her audience with anybody before. Think of it! Sharing that unbelievable devotion! At the curtain call, Judy literally shoved Liza right off into the wings, smiling, of course, as she did sometimes, that big, steely smile."

The Palladium concert was supposed to be a one-time performance, but since it sold out (even standing room), a second performance was added the next night. A live recording of the first concert was released as "Judy Garland and Liza Minnelli 'Live' at the London Palladium." It included solos by Judy ("What Now, My Love" and "Smile"), and Liza ("Gypsy in My Soul"), plus their duets and medleys.

"In two hours," Liza later recalled, "we went

through what most mothers and daughters go through over years and years — which was a daughter's discovery that she has a force within herself, and a mother's reaction to a daughter growing up. I was relieved that the audience liked me, and I could feel she was relieved that the audience liked me. By the end of that show, I knew I'd never be afraid to be on stage with anybody. If I held my own with my mother, I'm not gonna be afraid of anything."

The show also initiated a brief stretch of relative calm between mother and daughter.

"Mama's competitiveness disappeared immediately after the Palladium performance," Liza insisted, "and she fell into a period of unparalleled motherhood with me. Even to the point of introducing me to the man who later was to become my husband. I was attracted to Peter immediately. I had always been a person who reacted to others very quickly. I had to, because we moved around so much."

A month after they met, Liza and Peter were sitting in a restaurant with Mark Herron and Chris Bell. "We all were pretty high on those exotic drinks they served. Mama got up to go to the powder room and Chris went to make a phone call. Peter leaned across Mark and asked Liza not to go out with anyone else. Mark said, "To ask Liza to do that you have to be engaged."

Peter added, "All right, let's be engaged then."

Liza was so stunned she just shrugged. When Judy came back, Mark told her, "Guess what just happened. Liza and Peter are engaged."

"Mama was so thrilled, she started to cry," Liza recalled. Peter ran to his flat and came back with a cheap diamond ring he had picked up in Hong Kong. He put it on Liza's finger to find that it fit perfectly. Peter stood on a chair and announced their engagement to the entire restaurant, making it official.

Liza had to leave the next day for New York to try out for the lead in "Flora, the Red Menace," a part she desperately wanted. Maybe it was the charm of Peter's ring that helped her cinch the role, maybe not, but she got it. Five weeks later, Chris and Peter also arrived in New York.

Late in November 1964, Judy phoned the columnist Hedda Hopper from London to announce her daughter's engagement to Peter Allen.

"He and his brother, Chris (the two actually were not related), have a singing group that hit London like the Beatles hit America," Hedda assured her readers. She added, "Liza was leaving for Paris to get permission from her father, Vincente Minnelli. Judy phoned her special dress designer, Ray Aghayan, to do the wedding gown and trousseau. The date of the wedding has not been set, but Judy and Liza will be home within three weeks."

After work every night, Peter and Liza would meet in their cozy West 57th Street apartment and talk well into the early morning hours. He'd more or less been on his own since he was 13, which gave them something in common. Still, she was scared, constantly testing Peter and his love for her. He always passed, but every time they set a wedding date, something interfered.

"We had a couple of blowups," Peter later admitted. "I would move out for a while and Liza would stay at her girlfriends' a lot of the time. We were both working and we hardly ever saw each other, come to think of it. We were still so scared of each other — scared to commit."

But Vincente and his chic new wife, Denise, disapproved of Peter. He wasn't working, and Denise kept asking, "Just who is Peter Allen?"

Liza was torn apart. Peter said, "The only thing your parents have in common is you. They did something very good together when you were born, and they did it with love. But now I'm your family. If you really love me, we'll get married now and to hell with everyone else."

Possibly, Liza's hesitancy had something to do with her budding career. She opened on Broadway in "Flora" May 11, 1965, and the reviews were stunning. She was the youngest actress ever to win a Tony Award.

Lyricist Fred Ebb recalls that when Liza started out in "Flora," she was afraid to open her mouth. "Eight out of 10 ideas from her were terrible. It got to be a standing joke. Her fingernails were chewed up to her elbows." But he discovered that there was nothing temperamental about her. "She was great in the collaborative art that is theater."

After "Flora" closed, Ebb helped Liza put together a nightclub act.

"The essential thing about Liza is that she's an assertion of life," Ebb fondly added. "She went through scary, baroque, sordid things with her mother that I still find hard to believe. One push either way would have made her crazy."

Somehow she had come out of it, and that amazed him.

In September 1965, Liza made her nightclub debut in Washington, D.C., at the Shoreham Hotel's Blue

Room and she broke the club's attendance record. Later that year, Charles Aznavour would tell a French audience, "I've brought you a present from America." He called her "the American Piaf," and there were rumors that Liza and Aznavour were more than friends.

The next fall, Liza was off to Manchester, England. Albert Finney was directing and starring in the film "Charlie Bubbles," and he cast her in a small role as his secretary. The first-time director told the first-time actress, "Tone it down, luv, do half what you're doing." Liza was still such an unknown commodity that the voice of the movie trailer mispronounced her name, heralding, "Leeza Minnelli, mahvalous star of stage and TV, makes her own special contribution to 'Charlie Bubbles.' "

While Liza barreled from Broadway to Washington to Paris to England, Chris and Peter struggled with their show. She disliked his male friends and he disliked hers. Sometimes the only person she truly trusted was Fred Ebb. She was sure Peter misunderstood her devotion to Fred, just as she distrusted his coterie.

Chris and Peter appeared on the "Johnny Carson Show" and Carson liked them so much, he signed them for 22 shows. Peter dumped the leech friends of his whom Liza so disliked, and Liza finally committed. Their on-again, off-again engagement had lasted two years.

They were finally married March 3, 1967. Liza was 20 and Peter was 23.

Judy had managed to manipulate a young and naive Liza into marriage with a man she must have known was homosexual. Was she trying to ensure that Liza follow her own hard path? Whether she was pushed by Judy or made her own choice, Liza would soon find her life nearly a mirror image of her mother's.

Liza claimed she discovered the truth about Peter after their wedding, spending the night after the ceremony alone. It's more likely that she walked in on him during their two-year engagement. But Peter asked her to forgive him and promised to change.

Liza soon discovered she couldn't "adjust to normality." She had grown up on a roller coaster of highs and lows. There had been no middles, no tranquil time. "I was used to screaming attacks or excessive love bouts, rivers of money or no money at all, seeing my mother constantly or not seeing her for weeks at a time while she was away on locations. Now it was breakfast, lunch and dinner, marketing, shopping, consistency. Peter there, rock steady."

Peter tried to be all other things to Liza, if not a lover. He talked with her endlessly and helped her understand her mother. He also coached Liza to develop her singing voice. He would analyze her mistakes and make her acknowledge them.

Peter also became a true friend to Lorna and Joey, Liza's half sister and brother. Liza's apartment became a haven for them when Mama was in a bad mood and they needed protection and peace. Liza and Peter both believed that Lorna, at 14, had the real voice in the family, and they intended to help her in any way they could if she decided she wanted a career. Joey was only 12 and needed a man around. With his father, Sid Luft, battling Judy from the West Coast, Peter Allen became that man.

As protector, tutor and admirer, Peter was doing all the

things that any girl might want from a devoted daddy.

Judy was still all highs and lows, no middles. When her mother was in a low period and called her daughter, Liza just didn't answer the phone. Peter did. He took care of all their mail and paid the bills and kept her from going off the deep end over little things.

They parted for the first time when Liza went to Hollywood to film "The Sterile Cuckoo." Chris and Peter were performing at the Olympia Theater in Paris.

Liza had fought for two years for the leading role in the film. When she got the script, she sent it to Judy in London. Judy called immediately and asked, "But why do you want to play this? How could you possibly understand this screwed-up, neurotic girl?"

"Calm down, Mama," she said. "It's got nothing to do with you."

It was strange for Liza to return to Hollywood to make a movie of her own. Much of the city had changed since she'd lived there as a little girl. It was here that her mother enjoyed her greatest success and her most crushing defeats. It was here that Judy once told her, "I'm your best example of what not to do."

Mark Herron finally left Judy in April 1966 and returned to longtime lover Henry Brandon (with whom he remained until Brandon's death). Judy burned through a few more would-be rescuers before she arrived back in New York shortly before Christmas in 1968. She was planning to leave for London and a five-week appearance at the "Talk of the Town."

Judy renewed an acquaintanceship with Mickey Deans, manager of the popular disco Arthur. Mickey proposed, and they left for London December 27.

By January 9, they were married. Because of a legal snag, they married again in March in a Chelsea registry office, and celebrated with a reception at Quaglino's in London's West End.

Judy telephoned Liza to tell her she was getting married and to beg her to come to the registry and the party. "I'm sorry, Mama, I can't come to your wedding," she had said, "But I promise I'll come to the next one."

Liza says that, to her mother's credit, Judy "laughed so hard she screamed."

As always in the life of Judy Garland, this high was followed by a low. Judy was soon spinning out of control.

On June 22, 1969, after some 20 suicide attempts over the years, Judy Garland died alone in the bathroom of her London townhouse. There have been conflicting reports of the final hours and Mickey Deans' role in the tragedy. In any case, the coroner's report said that her death was caused by an "accidental overdose" of sleeping pills.

Liza and Peter were just concluding a summer weekend with friends in the Hamptons when a sobbing Mickey Deans reached Peter with the news. When Liza learned of her mother's death, she immediately called her godmother, Kay Thompson, who was living in Rome, to tell her that Judy had "joined the choir," which was Kay's way of saying someone had died. Although she had not seen Liza in eight years, Kay flew back to New York and remained by Liza's side, literally, throughout the funeral and in many ways, for the next 20 years.

With Kay's guidance, Liza and the kids got through the funeral. Newsreels of the period show a forlorn

Peter Allen, lingering awkwardly in the background while Liza huddles with Kay.

"The whole spirit of the funeral was directed by Liza," a friend recalled. "Everyone else really abdicated. Joy sounds like a strange word, but she felt the funeral should be joyous. She didn't want it to be somber and dreary."

Liza saw to it that Judy was laid out for the wake in the same lace dress she wore for her wedding to Mickey Deans. She tried to get Judy's favorite makeup artist from California, but he was working on the TV show "Green Acres" and its star, Eva Gabor, refused to let him go.

Liza decreed that her mother have a glass-topped casket and allowed the public to file past it all day. Twenty thousand mourners came to pay their respects under the watchful eyes of two guards.

Sid Luft wanted Judy to be buried in Hollywood, but Liza overruled him, insisting that her mother hated California. Mickey Deans suggested Ferncliff Cemetery in Westchester County, N.Y., where she was eventually laid to rest.

During the funeral, another tragedy took place unnoticed when a doctor was brought in to examine Liza and, after diagnosing tension and grief, prescribed Valium. Years later, after she emerged from the Betty Ford Center and was struggling with her drug addiction, Liza looked back at that moment and said, "I was so grateful that someone had given me an order, made a decision for me, that I did exactly as I was told. That was when it started."

Outside the Frank Campbell Funeral Home on Madison Avenue, thousands more spectators lined the street to catch a glimpse of the mourners. The funeral service was invitation only. James Mason, who co-starred with Judy so memorably in "A Star Is Born," delivered the eulogy. Afterward, everyone sang one of Judy's favorite songs, "Battle Hymn of the Republic."

Not long afterward, Liza dismissed in an interview the idea that psychiatry might have helped Judy — or herself.

"I'm not putting psychiatry down," she said, "but I just don't want to spend that much time with myself. I mean, well, I'm pretty content. If I go to a shrink, he might tell me some things I hadn't thought of about myself, and I might not like them, and I might not wake up the next morning."

Six years after Judy's death, Liza would still be claiming that life with her mother had been, if not conventional, full of love and support. She even tried to give her mother's more than 20 suicide attempts a positive spin. "I thought she would outlive us all," she said, "She was a great star and a great talent, and for the rest of my life I will be proud to be Judy Garland's daughter. She did everything she ever wanted to do, including those suicide attempts." Liza dismissed them as "just silly things to attract attention." She also insisted that her mother did not die of an overdose. "She just passed away, joined the choir, took a taxi, however you want to put it. She did it with style."

In those days, Liza's only regret about her mother's death seemed to be that Judy missed seeing her performance in "The Sterile Cuckoo," which opened Oct. 22, 1969. It earned her an Academy Award nomination.

Years later, when Liza herself was in rehab, she

would reverse her story, and tell fellow alcoholics at the Smithers Clinic that she was still tormented by guilt over her mother's death.

"Sometimes I would not even take my mother's calls because I knew she was loaded," sources say Liza told the group. "It killed me to ignore her, and it never stops haunting me that if I had tried harder, I could've saved her."

CHAPTER 3

Cover girl

"I never get mad. I'll chew Valium rather than throw a scene."

With Liza it was always love at first sight. That was how she fell for Peter Allen, and in the early 1970s she would make instant connections with Rex Kramer, Baron Alexis de Rede, Peter Sellers, Edward Albert Jr., and, most tragically, cocaine.

After her mother's funeral, the tyrannical director Otto Preminger offered Liza time off from filming "Tell Me That You Love Me, Junie Moon." True to form, she would have none of it and spent the rest of the summer of 1969 on location in Salem, Mass. She got through it with the aid of a Valium prescription and the constant presence of Kay Thompson, who had joined the cast in a small role. Liza's new friend, the designer Roy Halston Frowick, got a credit as assistant costume designer.

With Liza was a grizzled gray mongrel named Ocho that she had rescued six months earlier in an alley behind a San Juan bar called Ocho Puertos. "He's not a pet," she insisted. "We just sort of bumped into each other and are stringing along together. I just love him. He's so bored by everything."

When Liza returned to Hollywood, a friend who met her at the Polo Lounge noticed that she seemed haggard and distracted. She was drinking more scotch-and-Cokes than ever. He blamed it on the notoriously demanding Preminger.

Liza and Peter spent Christmas 1969 with Liza's father in Beverly Hills. Vincente had retired from MGM after more than 30 years. He was ailing, and his third wife was divorcing him. Peter liked Vincente, but complained that his father-in-law's life was an endless Hollywood social round.

"Night after night there was a party," Peter remembered, "with all the same people but in someone else's house, wearing different clothes but saying the same things over and over. Liza can enjoy that sort of thing. They've all known her since she was born and knew her mother and she makes herself enjoy it as an expression of loyalty to her mother."

It was different for Peter. "I nearly went out of my mind," he said later. "Everyone was so old. There was Jimmy Stewart and Cary Grant and Gregory Peck and all that age group. They're so dull to talk to. They've given up any mental stimulation and their brains have turned to butter." Peter told Liza, "I cannot bear one more night of this butter talk they go on with."

As far as Peter was concerned, Christmas in California was "the start of the big drift between us."

A few days after the holiday, Liza and Peter secretly separated. "When we decided to part, and did, it was a great weight slipping from my shoulders," said Peter said later. "I'm sure it was the same for Liza, so we are really good friends."

Peter was such a good friend that in the next few years he would stand quietly by as Liza romped through a series of wild affairs. As long as she was married to Peter, there was never any chance that the "engagements" she kept announcing would lead to marriage.

One of those engagements had come in November 1969, while Liza was visiting Houston, and friends brought her to the Bastille Club to hear a hot local quartet called Bojangles. When Liza was introduced to the band, she said to leader Ray Rogers, "You guys are great. Would you have any interest in joining my act?"

Soon Liza was flying Bojangles to New York to meet her agent, Stevie Phillips, at ICM. She was especially enthusiastic about one member of the group: boyish 21-year-old Rex Kramer, who played guitar, sang and wrote songs.

Rex Reed, who had known Liza since 1964, was among Liza's friends who viewed Kramer with suspicion. Reed described him as "like a baby-faced Beatle, with fuzzy hair, a soft Southern accent and lake-green eyes that don't miss a thing." Kramer, whose real name was Rex Kulbeth, had been married for two years and was the father of an infant son. He left them behind in Texas when the band headed for New York to rehearse for Liza's February opening at the Waldorf-Astoria. Peter was also still involved in developing the show, but others sensed that he and Liza were married in name only.

Liza seemed to like having her mature, calm husband and her playmate lover in the same room. This pattern would continue throughout her life.

After her sensational opening at the Waldorf's Peacock Alley, Rex and Liza were inseparable.

Bojangles was renamed American Sunshine and they traveled with Liza to the Concord Hotel in the Catskills, Constitution Hall in Washington, D.C., and El San Juan in Puerto Rico. By then everyone in the show knew that Liza and Rex were lovers.

"Rex was a super stud," Ray Rogers said of his band-mate. "And Liza made it very clear to us that he performed very well sexually and that was what she wanted from him. She and Rex looked as if they were terribly infatuated and they were all over each other in public, kissing and hugging."

Peter considered Kramer "an incredibly noisy hick" and did a devastating imitation of him. But he saw that his marriage to Liza was finished.

"Rex was exactly the opposite from me," Peter admitted. "He was a country boy who hated the city and loved girls. Liza enjoyed herself at first. She thought she was getting back to roots and after that she began talking about spending the rest of her life on his family's farm in Arkansas and eating black-eyed peas and grits. I knew she hadn't really gone country when she also mentioned that Ocho still ate only steak and caviar."

In March 1970, while celebrating her 24th birthday with Rex, she learned that she was being sued for $500,000 for "enticing him to abandon his wife."

Peggy Kulbeth sought a lawyer in Houston, Texas,

where alienation of affection was still a serious matter. In her suit, Mrs. Kulbeth charged that Liza had entered into a contract with Bojangles mainly as a way to assure Rex's company. She claimed that Liza, "by use of great power, wealth and influence, gained the affections of Rex Kulbeth and enticed him to abandon his wife."

Liza denied every allegation, saying she was not "the pursuer in this matter."

Liza got happier news at Cannes that May, when she learned that director Bob Fosse had won his battle to cast her in the movie version of "Cabaret." Four years earlier, she had auditioned 14 times for the Broadway show. John Kander and Fred Ebb had written the songs for "Cabaret" with Liza in mind, but producer-director Hal Prince considered her too American and, oddly enough, too good a singer. He refused to cast her and went instead with Jill Haworth in the role of Sally Bowles. It remains Haworth's one and only Broadway role. The show opened Nov. 20, 1966, and ran for almost three years.

Liza loved Bob Fosse's concept for the movie version, which was much truer to the original, gritty stories of Christopher Isherwood on which "Cabaret" was based. "We're trying to show the dirt and the decadence and the perverse atmosphere of Berlin when the Nazis came to power. All the musical numbers take place inside the cabaret, with real drag queens and cheap, tacky sets."

Liza's first three films had been straight dramas. She deliberately chose such roles because she wanted the public, once and for all, to realize that it was Liza Minnelli they were seeing on that screen, not Judy

Garland or Judy Garland's daughter. Now she was confident enough to take on a movie musical, especially a movie musical that Judy Garland could never have made.

"Cabaret" the movie was budgeted at a modest $3 million and would be shot in Germany to save costs. Liza arrived there in January 1971 with Rex Kramer, introducing him as her arranger-boyfriend and setting up in the artists' quarter of Munich. She told Rex Reed that Kramer was working with her on her music, easing her out of old standards and into a soft-rock scene. Liza assured Reed that when she was not working, "I spend all my time now down on the farm of Rex's grandparents in a little hick country town called Smackover, Arkansas. It's terrific."

Liza told Reed that in Smackover, people called her Liza May, and nobody thought of her as the daughter of Judy Garland. She didn't have to prove anything. She assured him, "When the movie ends, I'm going right back to the farm."

Kramer was said to be working on a documentary film about Liza. Unfortunately, like a lot of his plans, the film never happened. Liza later complained that he was becoming "madly possessive." He alienated not only the members of his own band, but also some of Liza's longtime musical advisers and was soon barred from the "Cabaret" set.

Liza and her assistant, Deanna Wemble, convinced Kramer that Liza had fallen in love with a cameraman. "He said he'd leave me only if I fell in love with somebody else. I knew he was using me," she said of the breakup. "I suspected that way back in Arkansas. First I thought, 'Oh, farms are the good life, the simple life,' only to discover that the good life ain't so simple. A month of it and you gotta say, 'OK, now out of the overalls, where's the action?'"

That need for action was what soon attracted Liza to Bob Fosse, her director in "Cabaret." A dancer in vaudeville at 13, Fosse had moved on to the Broadway chorus and MGM musicals of the 1950s. As a Broadway choreographer in the 1960s, he'd staged, "Sweet Charity," a showcase for his second wife, the red-haired dancer Gwen Verdon. The movie version of "Sweet Charity," starring Shirley MacLaine, had been a disappointment, however, and Fosse was determined to prove himself with the "Cabaret" movie.

A tireless womanizer, Fosse was drawn to the dark side of sexuality and drugs. As a father figure and a playmate, Fosse brought out the best in Liza, in "Cabaret" and later in her memorable TV special, "Liza with a Z." How he got those performances from Liza is still debated.

According to author Wendy Leigh, "Liza and Bob Fosse snort cocaine during the making of "Cabaret" . . . When his supply of the drug ran out, Fosse became demanding and impossible to deal with and the ravages of cocaine also took their toll on Liza."

Nevertheless, everyone involved with "Cabaret" worked to make the movie a success. Kander and Ebb contributed a new song, written originally for Kay Thompson, now tailored to her goddaughter. Liza and Gwen Verdon put together Sally Bowles's eccentric wardrobe by combing Paris flea markets.

Liza's co-star, Marisa Berenson, became a close friend. Marisa was Rex Kramer's total opposite. Through her friendship with Marisa, Liza became a card-carrying member of the glamorous international set that "Newsweek" would later label "the Marisa Mob." It included not only Liza, but David Niven Jr., Diane and Egon von Furstenberg, David De Rothschild, Paloma Picasso, Bianca Jagger, Helmut Berger, George Hamilton and Loulou De la Falaise, creative assistant to Yves Saint Laurent.

Marisa was the granddaughter of French fashion designer Elsa Schiaparelli, who coined the term "shocking pink." Her father, Robert L. Berenson, was a Boston Brahmin and career diplomat. "By the time I was 17, I'd seen half the world," said Marisa, "and knew everyone there was to know."

One story on the Marisa Mob noted that "even for the glamorous women in the Berenson set there appear to be precious few men to move in with these days."

With no one important in her life at the moment, Marisa turned to gay men, saying she had "become a big fan of homosexuals. I adore them. They are talented, sensitive, refined people who make the best friends. I'd rather go out with a fag than a boring man any day."

Her pal Loulou added, "There's nothing more fun than fags." Since Liza was the daughter of a homosexual and currently married to a gay man, the women had lots to talk about.

By the time "Cabaret" opened in February 1972, Kramer had retreated to Houston, playing small clubs and sounding battered by his affair with Liza. "The pace she sets for herself is simply terrific," he said, "but she just can't slow down. She would worry about not sleeping and would start taking downers to help herself." He described terrible tantrums, after which she would "literally rave, then collapse."

Liza denied Kramer's claims that she threw tantrums, but they sound suspiciously like the rages that other people, including her former stepmother Georgette and her sister Lorna, attribute to her in their memoirs.

In a final chapter to the affair, on May 21, 1973, Liza quietly settled his former wife's lawsuit out of court.

Rex Kramer, for the record, sank into oblivion. He made news again only on Nov. 8, 2001, when nearly two months after the horrific terrorist attacks that leveled the World Trade Center and damaged the Pentagon, he entered a bar in Deer Park and identified himself as a deputy U.S. marshal, showing what appeared to be a set of Marshals Service credentials. He told women in the bar that he was conducting an investigation and began asking them about anthrax.

"Because employees and patrons found Kramer's conduct bizarre," a U.S. Department of Justice press release explains, "they called the Deer Park Police Department." Kramer was arrested and officers found a switchblade knife and handcuffs on him. The next day they conducted a search of his home and vehicle. Inside the car they found a 9-mm pistol with two loaded magazines and extra ammunition. At his residence, they found instructions on how to fake identification, make a silencer and become a hit man. According to the press release, "Also found in Kramer's residence were more handcuffs, personal restraints, knives, blindfolds, ball gags, numerous packages of feminine hygiene products and lengths of rope, and a whip, and an unregistered .22-caliber rifle cut short to an illegal length with an operational homemade silencer."

Kramer pleaded guilty to impersonating a federal officer and other charges January 22. His public defender, Michael DeGeurin, argued for a lighter sentence, blaming his client's actions on "alcohol abuse stemming from his fall from fame as a former boyfriend of Liza Minnelli." Kramer was sentenced to 30 months in federal prison followed by three years of supervised release.

The whole time Liza was conducting her affair with Rex Kramer and rumors circulated about Peter's male friends, she insisted on presenting a picture of wedded bliss. She and Peter even cooperated on a lengthy cover story for Redbook, the popular family oriented-magazine. Redbook's Sam Blum emerged from his first encounter with Liza convinced that he had never met an actress "so constantly in control of the aspects of herself that she presented and withheld." He suspected that she used her dog Ocho as a prop to ward off troubling questions. When a conversation grew uncomfortable, she was likely to say, "Oh, look what Ocho's doing!"

Peter Allen was very present throughout the interview and seemed to Blum to be eager to help his wife. A weary amusement often crept into his tone as he described life with Liza. Asked what was important to his young wife, he answered, "Christmas. She drives me crazy with Christmas. She's very sentimental. She's all for flag and motherhood and that sort of thing."

Liza assured Blum that her husband brought her a red carnation once a week, and she made great fettuccini and the best pot roast in town.

As for children, Liza said she wanted to feel a lot more secure before she started a family. "I would love to be a champion parent," she told Redbook, "and I don't feel I'm prepared to be one yet."

Blum noticed that it was Liza who was more affectionate. Late at night her head would lean toward Peter's shoulder while he stared into space, his mind apparently miles away. While Liza was rehearsing one of his songs for her new album, he stopped her to say, "Too emotional." Uncomplaining, she tried it again.

"He's very strict," she said.

Liza's friends believed that Peter had been very good for her, in giving her great security and confidence in herself. Liza's career was beginning to eclipse his, but she and Peter insisted that neither of them had a problem with that. "I don't think I'm going to turn into an alcoholic if someone calls me Mr. Minnelli," said Peter. At the time, Liza was deeply involved with Rex Kramer.

Early in 1970, Liza was still assuring the press that she was still very much in love with her husband. "Peter is my rock," she said. "I love him. In fact, I like him. I really like him."

Peter didn't accompany Liza to the Academy Awards that year, although she was up for an Oscar for "Cuckoo." She almost didn't make it to the ceremony herself. She was riding with actor-producer Tony Bill on his motorcycle when he hit an oil slick on Sunset Boulevard. "The next thing I knew a big light was shining in my face, and a policeman was saying, 'you're going to be all right.'" Unconscious for an hour, Liza emerged to learn that she had a dislocated shoulder and 25 stitches in her scalp and would have to wear a back brace for months. She made it to the Oscars, however, with the help of makeup and painkillers.

Liza had been nominated as best actress for her performance in "The Sterile Cuckoo." Another daughter of Hollywood was nominated in the same category — Jane Fonda for her work in "They Shoot Horses, Don't They?" But it was Maggie Smith who won, for "The Prime of Miss Jean Brodie."

Just days after the Academy Awards, Liza and Peter announced their "temporary and amicable separation."

"It was just due to the pressures of trying to be a super-everything," said Liza. "It had nothing to do with the Oscars nor with the motorcycle accident." As it turned out, neither of them was in a hurry to get a divorce. Liza had fewer qualms about carrying on affairs knowing that her faux marriage protected her from having to make another commitment.

At the end of the summer, 1971, Liza suddenly had time on her hands. She had finished filming "Cabaret," she had dumped Rex Kramer, and her assistant, Deanna Wemble, had gone on holiday. For the first time in years, she had nowhere to go and no one to do it with.

Liza flew to Paris on a whim. She told her taxi to take her to the Plaza Athenee because that was where her father used to stay, and she called Kay Thompson back in New York. After Liza confided that she felt suddenly overwhelmed confronting her father's past, Kay advised, "Go instantly downstairs and out into the street and shout, 'Paris, you are beautiful, and so am I!'" It worked, and Liza could breathe again.

Next, Liza called her new best friend, Marisa Berenson, who was on her way to dinner at the Rothschild's and insisted that Liza come along. After dinner, Liza was introduced to the 48-year-old Baron Alexis de Rede, who reminded her that they had met earlier, at her opening at the Persian Room, which he'd attended with her former stepmother Denise. The baron wanted to see Liza again.

She soon flew back to New York for a consultation with Halston, the fashion designer she had met while working on "Tell Me That You Love Me, Junie Moon." Liza felt she needed clothes more appropriate for moving in high-society circles on the arm of the baron, and Halston provided a wardrobe for her adventure. His help solidified their friendship. Liza's fling with the baron would be brief, but her relationship with Halston would last until the end of his life.

The Baron de Rede, who had inherited a fortune from a male friend, lived in splendor in an apartment on the Ile St. Louis. An elegant figure, he was a fixture on the International Men's Best Dressed List. Liza was soon seen everywhere with him. In September 1971, they attended the Raffles Red and White Gala on the French Riviera. Wrapped in white Halston and wearing her hair cut boyishly short, Liza danced with the baron on a stone terrace of the Eden Roc Hotel. The baron never left her side, and even gave her a diamond friendship ring.

When Liza opened at the Olympia later that month, Baron de Rede gave a party in her honor in Paris. "I walked up the stairs," Liza said, "and they were decked with orchids and bathed in candlelight. When I walked into the room, ten violins started to play. Everybody in the world was there — Salvador Dali with his mustache twinkling, princes and clothes designers . . . St. Laurent . . . Richard Burton and Elizabeth Taylor. There was nobody who was halfway. Everyone was perfecto, just swell."

It was shortly thereafter that Desi Arnaz Jr. dropped in to see Liza backstage after she finished her act at the Riviera in Las Vegas at the end of 1971. Desi Jr. was the 19-year-old son of Lucille Ball and Desi Arnaz, whose TV series, "I Love Lucy," was an American institution, and his birth in 1953 was the most widely covered delivery in entertainment history.

Desi Jr. was considered mature for his age — sexually mature, that is. Two years earlier, after his affair with troubled former child star Patty Duke ended, she gave birth to a son out of wedlock. In 1971, it was generally believed that Desi was the father, although years later Patty, by then married to John Astin, revealed that John was the boy's father, but was married to someone else when Patty gave birth.

Desi Jr. was a sportsman, like his father. He had also been through a brief rock star phase as part of "Dino, Desi and Billy." (Dino being Dean Martin Jr.). His strong-willed mother welcomed Liza as a stabilizing influence on Desi. Besides, Lucy and Liza shared a love of dogs. Between them, Desi and Liza had seven dogs.

In January 1972, Desi won a Golden Globe as most promising young male actor for his performance in "Red Sky at Morning." By February, Liza was hinting that she might not work all that much in the future. With Desi she was discovering other things in the world, like tennis and skiing and backgammon.

"He is terrifically intelligent, and kind and funny, we are always laughing," she said. "And he is so mature for his age; like me, he sort of missed being a kid."

Desi Jr. had always worked and was becoming a fine actor. They thought they might even work on a project together. "Sure we'll get married," Liza assured an interviewer in February 1972, not mentioning that she was still very much married to Peter Allen. She would love to have children, but not just now. There was too much else to do.

The single best thing about Desi, said Liza, was that with him, "I do not have to apologize for being very good at what I do." There was also the fact that he was one of the best-looking young men in the business, which meant a lot to Liza, who was insecure about her looks.

Meanwhile, with the help of Bob Fosse, Liza was about to become a superstar.

"She has the ability to totally believe in a situation at any given time, which is what Judy had, too," said Peter Allen on the eve of "Cabaret's" opening February 13. "She's incredibly smart and intuitive, but she never intellectualizes anything. She'll push down her natural intellect to work with her emotions every time."

Liza presented a mixture of calm and frenzy, toughness and vulnerability. She chain-smoked, drank scotch and Coke, and bit her nails to the quick. She avoided scenes at all costs. She could not bear to be alone. Much of her endless energy seemed to come from nervous tension.

"Liza's philosophy is to be a moving target," said Peter. "But if you keep moving, things still continue to pile up. It's just more pleasant and so much easier to run."

At the end of February, Liza scored an entertainment coup, appearing on the covers of Time and Newsweek. It was the beginning of a kind of Liza-mania, as she appeared on the cover of every magazine that mattered for the next two years. Vogue and Harper's Bazaar battled to get her as a model.

"She was the '70s," said designer Joe Eula.

Liza attended the "Cabaret" premiere in New York with Desi Jr. and his father. She attended the West Coast premiere with Desi Jr. and his mother.

Desi Jr. was in Tokyo making a film called "Marco Polo" when he announced his engagement to Liza May 17, 1972. By then they were wearing identical gold friendship rings. Liza joined him there after she finished filming "Liza with a Z" May 31. Desi Jr. was eager to marry, but Liza sounded more cautious. "We won't get married for a while, but surely within the next few months."

Throughout the early 1970s, Peter Allen observed all these on-again, off-again engagements with amusement. Looking back years later, after they had amicably divorced, he recalled that "Liza kept announcing her various engagements in the Enquirer or somewhere, saying she was marrying — and I thought, 'Gee, we should get a divorce before Liza marries one of these people she's always getting engaged to.'"

Liza and Desi Jr. were on and off throughout the heady months of 1972, as Liza promoted "Cabaret." Desi Sr. announced that Desi Jr. and Liza would marry at his ranch in Las Cruces, New Mexico, and they appeared on Jack Paar's television show, discussing their romance.

Liza attended the 1973 Academy Awards with Desi

Jr. and her father, and Vincente's chic constant companion, Lee Anderson. Once again she had been nominated, this time for her performance in "Cabaret."

This time, she won. When Rock Hudson opened the envelope and announced that Liza was the winner, however, he added something like "this is a horse race and bloodlines count. Liza's got the bloodlines."

For Liza, this remark cast a shadow over what was, in many ways, her own shining moment. She had prepared an acceptance speech, just in case, but when she got to the podium she could not remember a word of it. Instead, she said, "Thank you for giving me this award, you've made me very happy." She had wanted to say so much more, she confided later, regarding how lucky she felt to be in an industry that supported her. Once again, Liza was living up to her parents' standards, rather than achieving success on her own.

Soon after the ceremony, Liza and Desi Jr. met with the press in London, where rumors of heavy drinking and loud quarrels followed them. They spoke freely — and quite frankly — about their love and respect for each other. John Lambert, of the Evening Standard claimed that he had been on his way to interview them in their hotel suite when she threw an empty vodka bottle at him from her window — missing his head by inches.

In early interviews, Liza is quoted frequently as saying that she hardly drank and never touched drugs. But the interviewers describe her chain-smoking Marlboros and drinking scotch-and-Coke or Grand Marnier. And Liza admitted in 1974 to one reporter, "I never get mad. I'll chew Valium rather than throw a scene. I enjoy behaving like a lady."

"She began taking five milligrams of Valium and a sleeping pill at night," according to one source. "By the time she starred in 'Cabaret' in 1971, Liza had moved on to stronger drugs. She was seen snorting cocaine with Bob Fosse during the movie's filming."

Rumors about Liza's drug use went as far back as her relationship with Rex Kramer. In her 1998 memoir "Me and My Shadows," Lorna Luft, Liza's sister, acknowledged that it was she who introduced Liza to cocaine. Lorna was 19 and Liza 26 when she took her into a restaurant bathroom to share a line of cocaine. In no time, Liza was hooked. Later, Lorna and Liza attended drug parties at the home of Sammy Davis Jr.

As early as 1972, during her affair with Desi Jr., there were rumors that Liza was overdoing it. One newspaper wrote, "Comparisons have been made between Liza's frantic lifestyle and that of Judy Garland, her talented and legendarily tormented mother."

Liza laughed it off. As for the rumor that she had "developed a penchant for pills," she insisted, "I don't even take aspirin."

At the end of 1972, Liza and Elizabeth Taylor were the only two stars featured in a special Life issue called "The Year in Picture." "Liza Minnelli emerged during the year as the long-legged girl w iththe flashing eyes and the green fingernails in 'Cabaret' — an outlandishly engaging performer."

Nothing did more to cement Liza's reputation in the press as a high-spirited party girl than her next adventure, the short-lived love affair with Peter Sellers.

Liza was still in telephone contact with Desi Jr. twice a day when she arrived in London in early May 1973. Kay Thompson was by her side. Liza was there for performances of "Liza with a Z" at three different venues: the Palladium, the Royal Festival Hall and the Rainbow Theater.

"Liza" kicked off at the Palladium May 11. Among the multitude of celebrities in the audience that night was Peter Sellers, 44-year-old star of "The Pink Panther," "What's New Pussycat?" and "Lolita." He had recently separated from both his third wife and his mistress and he was about to begin filming "Soft Beds, Hard Battles," in which he would play six roles.

Sellers found himself bewitched by 27-year-old Liza's performance. He visited her backstage, where he was even more smitten by her ebullient charm. They became lovers soon after, and Liza moved out of her suite at the Savoy and into his small London townhouse.

With reporters on their trail, Liza held a press conference to announce that her engagement to Desi was over. In a rambling, disjointed speech, Liza said, "The relationship has been deteriorating for some time — pleasantly. So there's no more engagement. That's been called off."

Instead, she revealed, she had met a wonderful man "and fell in love with him and I'm very pleased to say he fell in love with me too." That man, she said, was Peter Sellers.

Privately, Liza told friends that she had to cut herself loose. "I want to be free," she told them, "I don't want to be tied down." Back in Hollywood, Desi Jr. got the news about Liza's press conference on television.

He was described as being "stunned and bewildered."

Lucy tried to console him. "I told Desi when the breakup came, you cannot channel Liza ever, and you cannot domesticate her ever. And I knew that's what Desi wanted," said Lucy. "I love her very much, and I told Desi one day when he was at his lowest, 'I think I know how you feel dear, but I think I miss Liza more than you do.'"

Sellers could not tolerate the entourage that surrounded Liza, especially Kay Thompson. But they were her friends, and despite his objections, she was not going to get rid of them.

Then, after hearing astrologer-psychic Frederick Davies say on a radio program that Sellers and Liza shouldn't marry, Liza decided to speak with him. Sellers was furious that she had talked to Davies without him. He knew all the finest clairvoyants, astrologers and psychics in the world, he said, and she should have consulted him.

The last straw came one night when Liza playfully knocked off his toupee, and the love affair burned out in a few weeks.

"Yes, it's over," Liza said. "But I have no regrets. How can you regret anything that was so happy?"

Sellers, in black and looking pale, confirmed, "It's true, but it was for Liza to say so. We are finished. But it was not my wish."

On June 19, 1973, reporters found Liza at the London airport, on her way back to the States.

"I can't be a mother to him," she told them. "He's a charming man but absolutely impossible to be with. I couldn't take all his unpredictable moods. It's impossible to sustain a relationship with him.

We'd begun to battle too much." At least it was better to discover this after five weeks, she said.

If it had taken five months, or five years, to discover how wrong he was for her, "I would have been totally destroyed."

Desi Jr. was convinced that Liza never loved Sellers, but used him to break off their relationship. "Instead of being honest, she hurt and embarrassed me," he said, possibly with some truth.

When Liza returned to New York, the apartment she had been sharing with Peter Allen didn't seem right for an Academy Award-winning actress. With the help of decorator Richard Ohrbach, she tossed the old stuffy brown furniture and brought in bold yellow, red and orange. A bold "hot lips" sofa in vibrant lipstick red dominated the living room. The dining area became a tented niche for her grand piano, which doubled as a dining table. The decorator added a screen in one corner of her dressing room, so she could dress behind it while talking to company and never have to be alone.

Visitors recognized it all as a very Kay Thompson touch. As creator of the Plaza-dwelling Eloise, who was based on her goddaughter Liza, Kay had lived in a complimentary suite at the Plaza for years. New management had just ended her hat sweetheart deal, so she moved in with Liza, who was spending more time in Los Angeles and on the road than in her apartment.

By the end of the summer, Liza was seen around Beverly Hills with 22-year-old Edward Albert Jr. They had connected in January at the Golden Globe Awards ceremony, where Liza received the best actress award for "Cabaret" and Albert was named the most promising newcomer for "Butterflies are Free." (Just a year before, Desi Jr. received the same honor.) Albert was handsome, five years younger than Liza, and another Hollywood baby — the son of Edward Albert, who had starred on "Green Acres." He also preferred older women, saying, "I believe, as a woman matures, she becomes more female."

The romance with Edward Albert Jr. burned out quickly. Liza was constantly working and never home for more than a couple days at a time, so Edward moved on to Kate Jackson, a young actress who would soon star in the television series "Charlie's Angels."

During all this, Liza was still married to Peter Allen. "Our marriage is neither on nor off," he told reporters. " Liza and I are just better apart than together. We're still married, we see each other, we stay together when she's in New York. Life is different now. We can't go chasing off after each other. What eventually happens to us depends on what we both want and what we both get. Our careers are so dissimilar now, we don't move in the same circles at all."

While Liza made movies that took her to Germany, Mexico and Hollywood, Peter started performing in small clubs. Real-life cabaret was the medium that best suited him.

Liza came to his opening at the Bitter End in Greenwich Village, but she seemed as out of place there as he did at her father's Beverly Hills Christmas party. "She doesn't belong in Village clubs anymore," he said later. "Her life is in big movies and big TV shows.

"Neither of us wants a divorce," he went on. "We

both have other girlfriends and boyfriends from time to time and when we get together we talk about them, sometimes laugh about them. But divorce is not in the picture now. We are just best apart most of the time."

In November 1973, as Peter spoke to reporters, Liza continued to travel. Kay was producing and choreographing a historic fashion show at the Palace of Versailles. The idea was to demonstrate that American fashion was now equal to the fabled French couture. Judy Garland's old friend Eleanor Lambert, doyenne of fashion publicists, had suggested putting five American designers — Bill Blass, Stephen Burrows, Anne Klein, Halston and Oscar de la Renta — with five French couturiers — Yves St. Laurent, Marc Bohan for Dior, Emmanuel Ungaro, Pierre Cardin and Hubert Givenchy.

As Kay conceived it, the grand finale would bring all the American designers and models on stage at the same time, while Liza sang "Bonjour Paris."

With Halston, Kay and Marisa involved, there was no question about Liza's participation. Halston's models included her friend Elsa Peretti as well as Marisa. The aim was to raise money for the restoration of the Palace of Versailles.

Blass later recalled that "the bitchery and paranoia among the American designers, especially Halston and Anne Klein, nearly turned the whole thing into a disaster." Halston, flush with success, had become quite pompous. He traveled only by limousine and even started referring to himself in the third person, which amused Blass, who had known Halston since he was designing hats at Bergdorf's.

At noon on the day of rehearsals, Halston

announced that Liza would appear only in his segment and not in the "Bonjour Paris" finale. According to Blass, a livid Oscar de la Renta immediately got on the phone to Raquel Welch, who was making a movie in Spain, and begged her to be in his segment.

"I don't know what was worse for Liza to contemplate — her friend Halston's unsporting manner or the thought of being upstaged by a sex bomb — but she soon settled the matter," said Blass. Liza would perform "Bonjour Paris" as planned.

Halston then started verbally abusing Anne Klein, reducing her to tears. Disgusted with him, Kay walked out.

"Fortunately, she did not go far," wrote Blass. "Without Kay, in my opinion, to direct the opening number, we would certainly have perished in the flames of amateurishness."

The next day, the show began with the French. Each designer was allowed to show 10 outfits with limited props: a pumpkin for Dior, a rocket ship (which ran into a little trouble on take-off) for Cardin, a gypsy cart for Ungaro, a stretch limousine for St. Laurent. The French also had a 40-piece orchestra, Rudolf Nureyev, the nude dancers from the Crazy Horse and 70-year-old Josephine Baker herself singing, "It's Impossible."

Kay's presentation for the Americans was a blend of easy understatement and wild fantasy. Liza came out singing "Bonjour Paris," as all 50 American models, dressed in beige, paraded on a stage piled with luggage. The American presentation lasted only 35 minutes compared to two hours for the French, but it "brought the audience to its feet." Later Marc Bohan of Dior said, "After we saw the Americans, we looked like idiots."

Blass also noted that stars of Liza's stature were not permitted by their recording labels to actually sing for this kind of event. "Bonjour Paris" was lip-synched, marking the first time that Liza resorted to the controversial practice.

No lip-synching was ever included in the act of Jim Bailey, the famed female impressionist whose favorite subject was Judy Garland. Liza, who finally caught his act in 1973 after she attended the Paris fashion show, was stunned at the performance.

"When he is on stage, for me, it's like Mama is alive again." Liza was convinced that "Mama would have been the first to enjoy what he was doing."

This devotion to Bailey was something Liza shared with her sister. The first time Lorna heard Bailey sing, she couldn't believe it wasn't her mother. "I thought he'd played a trick on the audience — that instead of singing, he was miming to one of Mama's records."

Liza and Lorna would attend dozens of Jim Bailey's performances in the next few years. "Jim gives us something we just couldn't get from listening to Mama's albums," Lorna said. "When he's on the stage, it's like Mama's been reborn."

Liza urged Bailey to appear with her in a Las Vegas show. The idea was to re-create her Palladium appearance with Judy when she was 18.

"During rehearsals, Liza was fun," Bailey recalled. "But before the show, when I was getting ready and was already in my makeup as Judy, the door opened and I heard Liza saying in a trembling voice, 'Mama I have something for you.' All of a sudden I realized she was relating to me as her mother. It was eerie. She sat down next to me and handed me a small box. I opened it — and inside was a ring that Judy had once owned. I looked at Liza, and she said, 'It belongs to you, Mama.' And then she started crying as if her heart was breaking.'"

CHAPTER 4

Disco daze

"Give me every drug you've got."

Liza began 1974 with a sold-out engagement at the Winter Garden on Broadway. Rumors were flying that she was having an affair with Ben Vereen, who had been starring in the Fosse-directed musical "Pippin" for almost two years, but they denied it. After all, Vereen was a married man. Even so, they seemed to be everywhere, acting like a couple. They even posed nude together in a memorable shot taken by photographer Francisco Scavullo.

On the eve of her January 6 opening at Winter Garden, Liza sipped a scotch-and-Coke as she complained to columnist Earl Wilson, "If I go to a movie with somebody, they say it's a romance." She dismissed the gossip linking her to Vereen. "That's such an exaggeration. We're very dear friends. We should be. We're both proteges of Bob

Fosse's. I guess the man I date most is Bob Fosse."

Sparks may not have been flying between Liza and Ben Vereen, but they definitely were in the air between Liza and Jack Haley. Haley was a studio brat who at 6 years old, visited his father on the set of "The Wizard of Oz." Liza first met him when she was 14 and he was fresh out of the Air Force and seemed terribly mature. She didn't see him again until 12 years later, when she was involved with Desi Arnaz Jr. and Jack sought her out. He had just finished editing a film called "That's Entertainment!" and a major segment was devoted to Judy Garland. Jack wanted her daughter to introduce that section of the film.

At first, Liza didn't want to do it. She resisted anything that smacked of exploitation. But her father assured her that Jack knew what he was doing and encouraged her to have a look at his film. When she did, Liza was impressed, saying it was "beautiful, done with respect and affection." Haley also had enlisted Fred Astaire, Gene Kelly and Frank Sinatra, among others. Liza agreed to join these formidable stars to act as a "host." "That's Entertainment!" was an enormous success.

Before the film was released, Jack was producing the 1974 Academy Awards and he wanted Liza to open the show. Discouraged by her people, Jack went to Las Vegas, where Liza was working, cornered her in her dressing room and described the production number he had in mind: 40 chorus boys descending stairs in white tie and tails, with Liza out front. She immediately agreed to do the show.

Their relationship began as strictly business. Sure, she was attracted to him. Especially those big blue intelligent eyes — there was always something going on behind them. But ever since she was a small child she'd heard about Jack's reputation with women. She never dreamed he'd be interested in her that way.

Jack discovered that his idea of Liza was just as wrong. At that point, he saw her as the girl who flitted from relationships with Desi Arnaz Jr. to Peter Sellers to Edward Albert. It took some time for them to discover each other personally.

"We proceeded very cautiously," Jack told one magazine. "But, as one preconception after another began to fall away, we realized that we were very much alike — and not what we were reported to be at all."

After the Academy Awards, Jack began to pursue Liza, visiting her in Lake Tahoe to consult about a benefit event in which they were both involved. They stayed up for several nights talking about it after Liza finished her midnight show at Harrah's. The following night, he returned to Los Angeles. On April 15, Liza collapsed in the wings while waiting to go on at Harrah's. She blamed a recent bout of flu, but back in Los Angeles, Jack blamed himself.

On an impulse he called her and "started yelling at her," he recalled later. "What are you doing to yourself? You're not using good sense. I worry about you and I want you to start taking care of yourself." He insisted that she be his date at the May premiere of "That's Entertainment!" After that, they started dating seriously.

Until 1974, tall, genial, red-bearded Jack Haley Jr. was better known as an ingratiating raconteur than for any professional accomplishments. He was the son of Jack Haley, who had played the Tin Man in "The

Wizard of Oz," and Florence McFadden, a former
Ziegfeld Girl. Jack Jr. attended Loyola University and
studied filmmaking at the University of Southern
California and UCLA. He was photographed
frequently on the nightclub circuit, dancing with
starlets like Jayne Mansfield, and he was popular with
Hollywood royalty. In 1969, he was engaged to Nancy
Sinatra Jr., had been a longtime escort of Jill St. John,
and also had a long live-in relationship with former
Playboy Playmate Liv Lindeland.

His two attempts at feature films, Jacqueline
Susann's "The Love Machine" in 1971 and
"Norwood" in 1972, were failures.

But he had one great idea: a salute to the great
movie musicals. He began working on it while he was
at MGM, and the result was perhaps the greatest
movie montage ever. "That's Entertainment!" opened
in May 1974.

By July, Liza was staying at Jack's rambling
mock-Tudor house high in the Hollywood Hills. And
by August, lawyers for Liza and Peter Allen announced
that Peter had been granted an uncontested divorce
from Liza.

"When you've been separated longer than you've
been married, it's time to get a divorce," Peter said as
he signed the papers. As for the rumors linking Liza
and Jack, "I only know what I read in the paper," he
said.

Peter had released one album of his own songs,
"Tenterfield Saddler." Olivia Newton-John had a huge
hit with "I Honestly Love You," which he co-wrote.
He had started appearing at small clubs and cabarets,
many with a heavy gay following. He was working on

the songs for a new album, "Taught by Experts."
Friends wondered if he was talking about Liza. The
album also included a poignant salute to his former
mother-in-law, "Quiet Please, There's a Lady on
Stage."

While Peter was still struggling to establish himself
in this new career, Jack was having the greatest success
of his life. At New York's Ziegfeld Theater, "That's
Entertainment!" outgrossed even "Cabaret."

On Aug. 9, 1974, while Liza was appearing in
Allentown, Penn., she and Jack announced their
engagement. The headlines read "Dorothy's Daughter
to Marry the Tin Man's Son." Later that month
they arrived in New York to promote "That's
Entertainment!" Liza flashed her engagement ring: a
five-carat emerald surrounded by diamonds. "It's the
first jewel I ever had," she gushed. Vincente's new
girlfriend, Lee Anderson, threw a Porthault and
Baccarat shower for her in Beverly Hills.

Liza May Minnelli and Jack Haley Jr. were
married on Sunday, Sept. 15, 1974, at the historic,
Spanish-style Presbyterian Church in Montecito, a
small coastal village 90 miles from Hollywood. Only
nine people — all close friends and relatives — were
invited to attend. Shortly before the ceremony, a
smiling Liza showed guests her new gold bracelet set
with diamonds. "It's Jack's wedding gift to me," she
said. On the bracelet was inscribed, "I offer you all my
worldly goods, my name and my heart."

The following night, Sammy Davis Jr. and Vincente
hosted a "wedding celebration" for the newlyweds at
Ciro's, the legendary nightclub on Sunset Strip. The
men wore black ties while the women had 1940s-style

gardenia or camellia corsages. Sammy sang "Liza" to the bride, who was wearing a black velvet strapless Halston with matching choker and a real gardenia at her neck. Elizabeth Taylor was there in a silver lame caftan. Altovise Davis showed off the silver bugle-beaded gown that Marilyn Monroe wore in "Some Like it Hot." Eva Gabor was there, proving that Liza had forgiven her for refusing to loan her makeup man for Judy's funeral. Lucie Arnaz represented her family, demonstrating that the Ball-Arnaz dynasty didn't hold a grudge. Robert and Rosemarie Stack were there, too. Almost 30 years later, Elizabeth, Altovise and Rosemarie would also celebrate Liza's wedding to David Gest.

Liza insisted that her decision to marry was not impulsive. "Only a few times in your life do you feel — really feel — that you've found something absolutely right. I'd never had that feeling before; it was totally new to me."

Jack seemed so stable and grown-up emotionally. His own parents had been married for more than 50 years. A friend of his said, "Jack is completely secure, and there's no way he can be threatened by Liza. That certainly wasn't true of several of the men in Liza's past."

Liza admitted that she had spent a lot of time avoiding marriage until she found the right person. But Jack was a joy to live with. "And he understands me," she said.

They talked about having children, but not for two or three years, because of Liza's work commitments.

At home in Los Angeles, the Haleys liked to sit around watching TV and eating pizza. Liza was

looking forward to being the wife of the new president
of 20th Century Fox Television.

"Jack has business obligations which force me to put
on another hat. But I wear it pretty good," she said in
an almost rehearsed tone to an interviewer from Good
Housekeeping. "I get out the Baccarat crystal and all
that stuff, and I enjoy it because I like to make my
husband proud of me — not by performing but by
making things as perfect as I can for him in his home.
When he says 'I'm bringing so-and-so home for
dinner, it makes me feel good to have the table
beautiful, the music right, and to find out the interests
of our guests so the conversation will flow and the
atmosphere is never uptight.' To me, that's a big part
of being a woman."

By the time Liza sat for a cover story in McCall's in
February 1975, she was a genuinely bankable star. She
had been married to Jack for 21 weeks, and back only
four days from a series of one-night performances in
Europe. She was about to leave for Mexico, to begin
filming "Lucky Lady." While in Europe, her every
move had been material for the gossip columns, and
Women's Wear Daily obsessively reported on her tour
of Paris nightclubs with old pals like the Baron de
Rede. With an Oscar, a Tony and an Emmy to her
credit, she was in the same category as Barbra
Streisand.

Throughout the days of talks with reporter Barbara
Grizzuti Harrison, Liza was downing bull shots (vodka
and bouillon). A picture of Liza far less rehearsed than
in her recent Good Housekeeping interview emerged.
Rather than the content housewife, Liza appeared
more like a star spiraling out of control.

"They think I'm gonna burn myself up," she complained in frustration over the rotten scripts she was seeing. "They want to chew me up and spit me out while I'm still going strong. Well, that's their problem. You get yourself out before you get killed. I've heard all the rumors. I know they say I'm shooting up, pills — the whole works. How dare they? They're gonna try to grind me up. Well, I won't step into their grinder. They can make up a version of me — all I really am is an Italian broad — and put that version in their grinder."

Liza claimed that she had only just tried marijuana for the first time in Brazil. A "funny cigarette" was passed to her at a party. "I'd never tried it, and I said, Why not? Everybody else is doing it. I took a puff and nothing happened . . . three puffs, and I didn't think anything was happening. And then suddenly, oh, God, I saw everything and everybody that I didn't want to see." She was not going to go through that again. "I value life and I want to see it," she insisted. "And I'm not gonna do anything to mess it up."

Women's Wear Daily had just reported that "Liza Minnelli's steady date in Paris is no longer the Baron de Rede, but she is with a gang of Brazilian transvestite dancers." Liza was upset that the story implied there was something sexual going on between her and the dance troupe. She merely thought they were terrific artists and tried to help them drum up business for their show. She insisted that "the Baron de Rede was never my boyfriend, he's a friend of the Rothschilds, who are super good friends of mine, and we had dinner together, for goodness sake. And how could I have a boyfriend. I'm married!"

In the hour and a half that Harrison spent with her, Liza called her new husband Vincente once and "daddy" twice. It was clear to Liza insiders that although an older generation might regard Jack Haley Jr. as a playboy, his role in Liza's life was to be the daddy figure.

Vincente Minnelli, the man Liza really loved most in the world, was reaching the end of a long and illustrious career in films. From his directorial debut with "Cabin in the Sky" in 1942 until 1965, he had managed to turn out at least one picture a year. He had twice been nominated for an Academy Award, and won the Oscar for "Gigi."

His relationship with MGM had outlasted his three marriages, but in 1965, at the age of 62, he finally ended his association with the studio. "The Sandpiper," a 1965 vehicle for Richard Burton and Elizabeth Taylor, was his last movie with MGM. His first feature for Paramount, "On a Clear Day You Can See Forever," came in 1970 and starred Barbra Streisand, who had already won accolades for "Funny Girl" and "Hello, Dolly!" While he filmed this movie, his first wife, Judy Garland, died, and his third wife, Denise, left him for a San Francisco millionaire. "On a Clear Day You Can See Forever" was a disappointment at the box office.

Vincente had been trying for years to get a production going of one of his favorite novels. "Carmella" was a romantic, bittersweet story about an aging courtesan whose adventurous past is relived in the imagination of a young housemaid and confidante.

Liza did everything she could to help her father get his post-MGM career going, even throwing a party for him at the Greystone mansion when his memoir, "I Remember It Well," was published in 1974. She desperately wanted to make a movie with him.

Father and daughter were so determined to make "Carmella" that they never stopped to ask why every studio and distributor in town had turned down the project, even though it had an Academy Award-winning actress and her Academy Award-winning father attached to it. The difficulty lay in the material and the leads: an old woman, an old man (played by Charles Boyer) and a maid. The Minnellis pressed on.

Rejected by all the more prestigious studios, they were only too happy to make a deal with Samuel Z. Arkoff. A cheapskate and proud of it, Arkoff created a deal with Italian partners to finance the project. They would have to film in Italy, but Liza was just thrilled that her father's dream project would finally come to the screen.

Once she had realized her dream of working with her father, Liza kept to her typical hectic schedule, never sitting still. The next project to catch her eye was "Lucky Lady."

Stanley Donen, the movie's director, was a former dancer and came out of the Freed Unit that Judy and Vincente had been part of at MGM. Twenty years younger, he had eclipsed Vincente at MGM. Vincente's career lost traction after his 1959 Academy Award for "Gigi," while Donen's soared with "Funny Face," "Singin' in the Rain," "Charade" and "Two for the Road." His career had since slowed down. His last two films had been "The Staircase," in which Richard Burton and Rex Harrison played bickering longtime lovers, and

"The Little Prince," Lerner & Loews's last musical.

Liza was as excited as Stanley Donen about "Lucky Lady." It had taken her three years to find a role to follow "Cabaret." This was it.

"I love the part," she said. "It's the best script I've read since Cabaret." She'd play Claire, a gunrunner's sidekick. "She's a tough red-haired cookie who gets caught in the dream of money, money, money."

There were problems from the beginning. George Segal, who was to play Kibby, became ill and had to be replaced in a frantic scramble. Gene Hackman was the best actor available, but he insisted on being flown home to Los Angeles every weekend and did not mix with the cast and crew on location in Mexico.

There were rumors that there was a lot of mixing going on there, too. The obvious conclusion would be that Liza had taken up with her co-star, Burt Reynolds, who had just ended a long relationship with TV star Dinah Shore. In fact, it was not Liza but kid sister Lorna, now 22, who fell for Reynolds while they were on location. Liza was already more interested in Martin Scorsese, who visited her in Mexico to talk about her next movie project: "New York, New York."

When Liza returned from months on location in Mexico, Jack celebrated with a gala bash July 26, 1975. One side of the invitation pictured Liza with the message "Liza's back!" scrawled on her bare back.

Some 120 well-wishers gathered at Chasen's. A radiant, barefoot Liza appeared in a red Halston, complete with turban and flowing scarf that she twirled around her head in the style of Kay Thompson. "I always wanted to go to Chasen's barefoot," she quipped, "and when it's your party, you wear what you want."

Liza bounced around the room, stopping only to kiss actor David Janssen and chat with guests. When she knelt to speak with Altovise Davis and Shirley MacLaine, a photographer got a shot of the blackened soles of her feet, a sharp contrast to the ultra-posh decor.

The surprise hit of the evening was the appearance of Burt Reynolds, with Lorna as his date. They stayed 15 minutes.

Liza sang at the piano. She laughed and ran to the waiting arms of her husband. The merrymakers, who included Frank Sinatra, Gene Hackman, Ryan O'Neal and his little daughter Tatum and Raquel Welch, celebrated far into the night.

In July 1975, John Kander and Fred Ebb's new musical, "Chicago" directed by Bob Fosse and starring Gwen Verdon and Chita Rivera, opened on Broadway. A month later, Gwen was hospitalized with a throat ailment. She would be out for five weeks. The show would never last that long without a major star in the role of Roxie Hart.

Liza had not played on Broadway in 10 years, but when her friends asked her for help, she didn't hesitate. On August 8, she went into the show after barely a week of rehearsal and kept it afloat until Gwen returned. A grateful Fred gave Liza a gold Lifesaver charm.

Liza's next project was "A Matter of Time," an unmitigated disaster that was all the more heartbreaking because it was tied to her father's incompetence. Without the support and resources of a giant studio, Vincente was lost. Because they were filming in Rome and Venice, he was working with unfamiliar crews in a different culture. Italy was riven by labor problems and the set was hit frequently by strikes. Production fell behind schedule immediately, and that added to the pressure to complete the movie as quickly as possible. Even the weather was against them: record cold temperatures and rain. Liza sought escape every night in the Rome nightclubs, often with Lorna, who came over to visit.

Even after the film wrapped, the trouble wasn't over. Vincente's mental powers were failing. By the time he started the editing process back in Los Angeles, he had lost control of the material. He took forever to come up with a final cut, and when Arkoff, who had once again backed Vincente, took a look at it, he was furious. Arkoff secretly asked Jack Haley Jr. to try to salvage it. It's unclear whether Liza and her father knew that Jack edited their picture. In any case, they were furious that it had been taken out of Vincente's hands and blamed Arkoff for the mess that was finally released and quickly forgotten.

At the beginning of 1976, Liza was struggling to save "Lucky Lady" by making promotional appearances, and to finish "A Matter of Time." But there were still bright projects on the horizon. She was committed to Scorsese's big-band saga, "New York, New York," and she hoped to do the movie version of "Chicago."

"After that," she said, "I'll get the family."

Scorsese was small and frail, having suffered all his life from severe asthma. The director who had established himself with "Mean Streets," "Alice Doesn't Live Here Anymore" and "Taxi Driver" was, like Liza, insecure about his appearance.

"Taxi Driver" had won the Palm d'Or at the

Cannes Film Festival in 1976, but for Scorsese, winning the coveted prize was also the beginning of a crash. According to Peter Biskind, author of "Easy Riders, Raging Bulls," Scorsese once said: "It was a few weeks after the night when 'Taxi Driver' opened (Feb. 8, 1976) that I remember I started playing with drugs . . . For me it was just the beginning of going to an abyss for about two years and coming out of it just barely alive."

Scorsese moved on to an even more ambitious project with United Artists. "New York, New York" was going to be a totally new kind of Hollywood musical. Scorsese thought it would be a big-budget homage to the musicals of the past, "a cross between Vincente Minnelli and John Cassavetes." It would star Liza and Robert De Niro.

The movie went into production without a finished script. Scorsese knew the script wasn't ready, but he had gotten "a big head," as he recalled after the fact, and assumed he could "work it out on the soundstage." Looking back, he says, "A lot of guys work that way. Evidently I couldn't."

They filmed the "Happy Endings" number at MGM. "It was extraordinary," Liza said later, "because all of the people who worked at Metro so long and are still there — the grips, the people I'd known all my life — all came to watch this production number. It was, oh, it had a wonderful feeling about it. It was like Metro came alive again for two weeks."

The 12-minute showstopper began with Liza as an usherette at a movie palace shining a flashlight on her face like a spotlight and singing about happy endings in the stars, but maybe not for her. It even featured a cameo by her father-in-law, Jack Haley Sr., a veteran song-and-dance man. It was a knockout piece of filmmaking with glittery sets, huge crowds and swooping crane shots. Producer Irwin Winkler would later deny rumors that the sequence alone cost $1.2 million and said it was closer to $350,000.

Scorsese later admitted that during the entire production of "New York, New York," he used cocaine as a creative tool. "I didn't know how to get to these feelings. I kept pushing and shoving and twisting and turning myself in different ways, and I started taking drugs to explore, and got sidetracked a lot of the time. We put ourselves through a lot of pain." At one point, Scorsese kept over 150 fully costumed extras waiting while he talked to his shrink from his trailer.

According to Biskind, although Scorsese's wife was pregnant, he and Liza began carrying on an open affair. After his wife gave birth to their daughter Domenica, he left her.

Principal photography on "New York, New York" was completed in August 1976, but Scorsese's job was really just beginning. He now had to edit it down to a reasonable length. Four months later, Scorsese was still struggling to finish the movie. His first film editor had died. When he begged Marcia Lucas to take over, she left off working on her husband George's "Star Wars" to help out Scorsese. Lucas himself stopped by Scorsese's editing room. According to Biskind, "he told Marty that he could gross an additional $10 million if De Niro and Minnelli walked off into the sunset a happy couple instead of going their separate ways."

Scorsese could not bring himself to give the picture that kind of ending.

By early 1977, word on the street was that "New York, New York" was a masterpiece. Lush sets, dazzling production numbers and a sophisticated unhappy ending. Marcia Lucas told her husband, who had just completed "Star Wars," 'New York, New York' is a film for grown-ups. Yours is just a kids' movie, and nobody's going to take it seriously."

At a press conference in January 1977, Liza described the rumored anarchy on the set. "I think back and I don't know how any of us survived it," she said. "The energy level that went on was just incredible, and my own energy level isn't exactly zilch, as you know. This is the only movie I can remember making where I can't remember ever sitting down. It was like a whirlwind."

At that same press conference it became clear to reporters that Liza had been locked out or at least ignored by De Niro and Scorsese. One observer said, "Minnelli always seemed to be the last to find out what was going to happen when the camera rolled." Another described De Niro's performance as "a virtual circus of horrors that seems bent on upstaging Minnelli."

After the movie's premiere June 21, 1977, there was a party at Studio 54. Scorsese's brother showed up and began verbally attacking him. It was a bad omen.

Early in 1976, Jack Haley Jr. still sounded madly in love with his bride. He even seemed to understand her restlessness. "Liza has truly lived out of a trunk since her mother's marriage to Vincente Minnelli broke up," he said. "A home is what she really wants — and what we're going to have. She's never known any roots and she needs some now."

Liza sounded just as committed. "I didn't get a divorce until I fell in love with Jack," she explained. "He's a good Irish lad, and our life together just works. I wouldn't have married otherwise."

But both of them had been too busy with their work to go house-hunting in Los Angeles. They were still camping out at Jack's elegant but cramped bachelor quarters in the Hollywood Hills.

In January 1976, after spending six weeks in Rome filming "A Matter of Time," Liza took time off to promote and, she hoped, salvage "Lucky Lady." Stanley Donen had considered two different upbeat conclusions to replace the original dark ending in which Liza's two rum-running partners (Burt Reynolds and Gene Hackman) died. Needing a $30 million gross to break even, Donen patched together a happy ending that no one liked.

"They cut the guts out of the film, its emotional weight," Liza complained. Donen had turned it into a second-rate production, in her view. Burt Reynolds supported her, adding that Donen's final cut had "cheated Liza out of an Academy Award."

Possibly Liza was worried about the rising tide of stories that she was abusing drugs. Moving to squelch rumors, Liza cooperated with a January profile in People magazine that assured readers that "Judy Garland's daughter pops no pills stronger than Valium. She is fond of bull shots at lunch, but she dilutes her nightly scotch with Coke. She no longer chain-smokes but has failed to kick completely her Marlboro habit." Acrylic nails, the writer went on to mention, were helping Liza break her lifelong nail-biting habit.

In 1975, Liza's friend Halston had taken over a

four-story carriage house with a three-story living
room at 101 East 63rd Street. By 1977, it had become
the center for parties and intrigues among the crowd
that Women's Wear Daily dubbed the "Halstonettes."

On May 2, 1977, Halston's friend, the set designer
Joe Eula, dragged him to a new club, Studio 54. It was
love at first sight. Studio 54 became the designer's
second home, especially after host Steve Rubell
invited him downstairs to the shabby but super-
exclusive basement room — a secret hideaway of sex,
drugs and disco enjoyed only by the ultrachic.

"A Matter of Time" had by then become an even
greater disappointment than "Lucky Lady" to Liza.
Even so, she had every reason to believe that things
would turn around. For one thing, she and Marty
were far from alone in believing that "New York, New
York" was going to be a masterpiece. Regarding their
rumored affair, they followed the traditional public
practice: deny, deny, deny. Privately, Scorsese's wife
fumed and Jack fretted.

Liza was so deeply involved with Scorsese and his
working style by now that together they decided that
he was the only man to direct her return to Broadway.
On Jan. 25, 1977, it was announced that Martin
Scorsese had been lured to the stage by the new Liza
Minnelli musical. At the time, the title was "In
Person"; it later became "Shine It On;" and it finally
arrived on Broadway as "The Act."

George Furth had written the show especially for
Liza, and John Kander and Fred Ebb would reunite
with her for the songs. Rehearsals were to begin in late
spring, and the show was due in New York by late
October after West Coast engagements. Although it

had all the makings of a Broadway smash, by the time
the show opened — after three titles and two months
of tryouts in four cities — it was a critical disaster and
a shambles of overworked material. All it ever had
going for it was Liza's high-voltage presence.

Because she was in Detroit with "The Act," Liza
could not attend the 1977 Academy Awards on March
28, but her husband and lover crossed paths at Dani
Janssen's traditional Oscar night party. After the
ceremony and the many parties, Scorsese gave a lift to
Andy Warhol in his limousine at two in the morning
and then headed back alone to the dark, deserted
MGM lot to edit "New York, New York."

Days before the movie premiere, Scorsese and his
wife hosted a wild family-style dinner party for their
friends, including Liza and Jack at the Sherry
Netherlands. The much anticipated opening of "New
York, New York" came June 21, 1977, and was
followed by the traditional party at the Rainbow
Room. At 1 a.m., the survivors moved on to a second
party at Studio 54. A band played the movie's theme
song as Liza was carried in. The theme played again as
they brought in Scorsese. At 10:00 a.m., Liza caught a
flight to Los Angeles to resume rehearsing "The Act."

"An overwhelming friendly climate of opinion
awaited 'New York, New York,' " wrote Gary Arnold
of the Washington Post. "Scorsese has squandered it."
De Niro's Jimmy Doyle, a jazz musician, seemed
more boorish than sexy or amusing. Liza's Francine
Evans, a band vocalist, seemed more slow-witted than
desirable. Did Liza have any clue how unflattering her
costumes were?

Scorsese had cut Liza's 12-minute "Happy Ending"

number, removing even Jack Haley Sr.'s cameo, and reducing it to a three-minute shadow of itself. He removed or truncated many of the musical numbers and chose instead, to keep endless scenes of De Niro's improvised dialogue.

"The Act" opened in Chicago July 4 to unanimous pans. One headline, "Liza with a Zero," spoke for the majority. The show immediately became the focus of national coverage. Audiences hated Liza's costumes by Theodora van Runkle. One critic called them "sadistic." Liza threw them out after the first performance and pulled some sequined Halstons from her closet.

Liza sang all 14 of her songs with a microphone in her hands, still a controversial practice among musical theater purists, who expected their singers to be heard in the back of the hall without any help. Even worse, word was that a number of her songs were prerecorded and lip-synched. Several customers complained that they had not paid $20, then top dollar, for a ticket to see Liza lip-synch. The show itself was "an absolute nightmare," "unendurable" and "a colossal disaster."

The only two people who didn't seem to realize this were Marty and Liza. Despite their denials, sources say they were still very much involved with each other. Inside the troubled production, the musical's authors, Furth, Kander and Ebb, threatened to quit unless Scorsese was removed. It's a measure of Scorsese's hold on her that Liza was willing to jeopardize her relationship with Fred Ebb by making a stand on her lover's behalf.

After the San Francisco show also bombed, the producers tried to bring in Michael Bennett, creator of

"A Chorus Line" and widely regarded as a genius at fixing shows. Liza would not allow it. "What actress with any sense of reality would turn down an offer from Michael Bennett to restage a show that had been blasted in both Chicago and San Francisco?" asked one critic. "Only an actress personally involved in a romance with her mentor."

The stress was taking its toll. According to one report, Scorsese needed medical help twice in Chicago. Once a doctor visited him, and the other time he was hospitalized. When reporters asked why, they got two different answers. Some said it was Scorsese's asthma, but insiders believed that he had a problem with cocaine.

Liza's contract for "The Act" gave her final say on everything, including the director. Many of the veterans involved in the show wanted Scorsese fired, but by September they concluded that having him around was a good thing. "It's like she's out there working for him," an insider told Newsweek. "The only problem is that she's excessively loyal to her men. She loves, perhaps, too blind, and that's where she comes close to the story of the show."

Liza was playing Michelle Craig, a 31-year-old actress-singer-dancer whose movie career was on the skids. The show began with her doing the opening number of a big comeback act at a Las Vegas hotel and suddenly shifted to events in her past life, continuing to alternate back and forth throughout as she encountered her ex-husband producer, her ex-lover and her confidant. During the strenuous two-and-a-half-hour performance, Liza was the only one who sang, and she left the stage for only four minutes. The rest of the time she was giving her all to the audience.

Jack and Liza tried to squelch the rumors that she was having an affair with Scorsese by holding hands at the Bistro in Los Angeles at the opening-night party for "The Act." Scorsese, whose wife had recently filed for divorce, remained on the other side of the room all night.

After Scorsese suffered another asthma attack in September, Gower Champion finally stepped in as director.

"Did you ever have trouble with a show?" asked one shell-shocked insider who had been involved with "The Act" from the start. "Double that, and you're not even close to what we've been through."

"The Act" opened October 29 in Manhattan at a gala premiere. Elizabeth Taylor's arrival with her new husband, John Warner, almost caused a riot, and when Sammy Davis Jr. and his wife, Altovise, emerged from a limousine, the crowd rushed the barricades. Also among the celebrities at Liza's opening was Ruth Warrick, long-running star of the daytime drama "All My Children." Ruth would make a reappearance in Liza's life after her marriage to David Gest, describing how he had proposed to her but she had turned him down for fear he was gay.

Jack Haley was by Liza's side at the party at Tavern on the Green, while Scorsese lurked on the edges of her eight-member party. Jack once again laughed off the rumors. "Desi Arnaz Jr. was here, too!" he said. He gave his wife a 14-karat gold "Valium" pill as an opening-night present.

If "The Act" was a big hit — and how could a Liza Minnelli musical miss? — she was committed to staying in New York until July 4, 1978, and Liza hinted that she might even consider staying longer. It meant that she and Jack would live in Manhattan for a while.

They started apartment-hunting and discovered that co-op boards were notoriously hostile to people in the entertainment business. After being turned down by the board of the posh River House, they opted to acquire the designer Kenneth J. Lane's townhouse. The five-story brownstone in the quiet Murray Hill neighborhood had four bedrooms, four fireplaces and a beautiful secluded garden.

Unfortunately, Liza's second marriage would break up before she got to move in.

By November, Liza had begun a relationship with the notoriously virile ballet star Mikhail Baryshnikov. His interest could not have come at a better time. Theater insiders were reeling from John Simon's attack on Liza's appearance. The New York magazine theater critic had always been tough, but he outdid himself in his review of "The Act," focusing with distaste on Liza's face, which he described in the harshest of terms. For a woman who had always been insecure about her looks, it could have been devastating, but Liza could console herself with the knowledge that Misha, one of the most desirable men in New York, was crazy about her.

Baryshnikov was a glamorous figure, and unlike Rudolf Nureyev, Misha loved women. Born in Latvia in 1948, he was already a star of the Kirov Ballet before his daring defection to Toronto in 1974. He was now a member of the American Ballet Theater. His first love was prima ballerina Natalia

Makarova, but there had been many others since.

Liz Smith broke the news of the sizzle between Liza and Baryshnikov in December 1977. He was seen hanging around backstage at "The Act" and he and Liza were seen going in and out of Studio 54 together.

The strain of maintaining relationships with Scorsese and Baryshnikov, and the late nights at Studio 54, especially the sessions in the basement room, didn't help Liza's always fragile health. She missed seven performances of "The Act," and since there was no understudy, those performances had to be canceled.

If Liza made any resolutions to clean up for the New Year, she quickly forgot them. On January 3, 1978, Andy Warhol wrote in his diary about a story Halston had told him. Warhol recounted that Liza arrived at Halston's Upper Eastside townhouse, a hat pulled down to hide her face, and said to Halston, "Give me every drug you've got."

Halston told Warhol that he gave Liza a package that included Valium and Quaaludes.

Two weeks later, Jack Haley Jr. seemed very much on the sidelines as he scanned the crowded dance floor at Studio 54 and watched his 31-year-old wife get swept up by the 6-foot-4 dancer Sterling St. Jacques. "Studio 54 today is like the Stork Club in my day," he said, perhaps acknowledging that his wife belonged to another era.

Haley made the comment to Washington Post fashion reporter Nina Hyde, who noticed that a man in green was sniffing something, possibly cocaine, and others were sharing nasal inhalers associated with poppers. But when she asked the club's 33-year-old co-owner, Steve Rubell, he assured her, "When I see people using drugs, I ask them to stop. But I'll admit I don't always see them."

By January 17, Liza had missed 13 performances of "The Act" and blamed a lingering virus. She had moved out of the Central Park South penthouse she was sharing with Jack and into a hotel suite.

"My doctor advised me to keep away from anybody I didn't want to give the flu to," she said. "Of course there's no separation. I don't want to give him what I got."

Jack also publicly scoffed at separation rumors. Privately, however, he expected Liza to shape up.

Their stories often conflicted. Liza told one reporter that Jack was coming back from Detroit to take her to the hospital, but the reporter found that Jack was already in New York and planning to take in a concert at Carnegie Hall. Liza didn't seem to know her husband was back in town. "She was just confused because she's so sick," Jack said smoothly. "With a sick wife, I'm not going to any concert."

Liza blamed her exhaustion on "The Act's" schedule. No one else in a Broadway musical was doing what she did in eight shows a week. She was convinced everything would be fine if the producers would just let her out of matinees. They could not afford it, they said, but agreed to close the show for two weeks so their star could get some rest at a spa in Texas.

Liza denounced rumors linking her to Baryshnikov. "They're trying to ruin us," she said. But privately, Haley was said to be growing weary of playing the loyal, long-suffering spouse. Friends urged him to stay, pleading that Liza needed his stability.

Halston's townhouse soon became a refuge for Liza, whose life was "very complicated now," Halston explained to Warhol. For example, she had been walking on a New York street with Jack when they ran into Scorsese, who confronted her about her affair with Baryshnikov. Still, a week later, on January 9, Jack was with Liza's group at the 21 Club when she posed smiling between Bianca Jagger and Jacqueline Onassis.

When Liza returned to New York at the end of January, Warhol noted in his diary that Baryshnikov was waiting outside Halston's townhouse while Liza was inside, asking Halston if she and Baryshnikov could spend time at his place. "Liza and Baryshnikov were taking so much cocaine," Warhol noted in his diary. "I didn't know they took so much, just shoveling it in." Warhol found it "exciting to watch two really famous people right there in front of you taking drugs, about to go make it with each other."

By February, Halston was awash in cash from his deal with the Norton Simon conglomerate. He moved his headquarters into the Olympic Towers on Fifth Avenue at 51st Street. The salon's 20-foot ceilings, floor-to-ceiling windows, and golden panorama of the south, west and north skylines, made a sensational backdrop for fashionable clients like Liza and Elizabeth Taylor. Liza modeled at his opening party while the sound system blared her recording of "New York, New York."

Jack moved out of their Central Park South penthouse, and on February 25, the front page of the

New York Post announced that he and Liza were separating.

As usual, there was no time for mourning. On March 12, Halston threw a party for Liza's 32nd birthday at Olympic Towers. Liza wore a gold Halston dress that Warhol described as "open from the crotch down to the floor in a V." Scorsese was there with Robert De Niro, who had fattened up for his role in "Raging Bull." Also on the scene were Al Pacino, Truman Capote, Diana Vreeland, Martha Graham and Carol Channing.

Bianca and Steve Rubell brought out an enormous birthday cake, and Liza sang "New York, New York." Sterling St. Jacques tried to join her, but, according to Warhol, "she got upset and moved to another microphone."

On April 18, 1978, Haley called it quits and filed for divorce in Santa Monica, citing "irreconcilable differences."

Soon Liza's relationship with Baryshnikov also disintegrated. She was next linked to David Bowie, Al Pacino and John Travolta, but Halston remained the most constant man in her life and drugs continued to be the driving force.

Liza did not seem to be suffering as she joined Halston in saluting Studio 54 on its first anniversary party April 26. Halston congratulated Rubell and Ian Shrager for all they had done for New York. Warhol and Bianca both gave speeches. Liza, in red Halston, sang a new song from "The Act." Bob Colacello of Vanity Fair told Warhol that he had not heard such self-indulgence by a clique since Hitler's bunker.

All that cocaine was starting to take a toll on some

of those closest to Liza. Halston was having trouble with his next season's line. Paranoid, distracted, unable to work, he blamed his eight-member household staff and fired them all. There was an ugly, drunken scene between him and Elsa Peretti in the basement room at Studio 54. Noted Warhol, "Halston's really a wreck."

Author Wendy Leigh said that sometime in the late 1970s Liza was seen on a wild drug binge on Fire Island. "Liza looked horrible and was on cocaine for four days. They had a barbecue and the only thing Liza touched the entire time was hot dogs, champagne and tons of coke."

Liza was with Baryshnikov at Studio 54 when Halston asked Warhol to show Liza her portrait. The four of them went to Halston's new Olympic Towers studio. "They loved the paintings," Warhol recorded in his diary. "Baryshnikov talked about them for hours." But Warhol also noticed that Misha "only likes every girl for a minute." By November the dancer had moved on to Jessica Lange, with whom he would have a daughter.

By April 1978, Scorsese was busy with "Raging Bull" and had found his next wife, model Isabella Rossellini, the daughter of actress Ingrid Bergman and director Roberto Rossellini. Isabella had made her movie debut in a tiny role in the Minnelli fiasco "A Matter of Time."

The new couple attended the Telluride Colorado Film Festival, where Scorsese started coughing up blood and blacked out for the first time in his life. According to author Biskind, after returning to New York, he was admitted to New York Hospital, where a doctor warned that he was bleeding internally and could suffer a brain hemorrhage at any second. He was down to 109 pounds.

After the doctors saved his life, Scorsese got the message and cleaned up. He and Rossellini were married in Rome on Sept. 30, 1979. A former girlfriend joked that Scorsese was sleeping his way through the daughters of his favorite directors. Rossellini divorced him in 1983, complaining, "He wanted me to spend life between the cookstove and the kids."

Liza, meanwhile, was nominated for a Tony Award as best actress in a musical. By the time she and the company of "The Act" performed the "City Lights" number at the Awards on June 4, the best escorts she could find were Halston and Steve Rubell.

Rubell's party was also coming to an end. In December, armed IRS agents raided Studio 54 and seized records and cash hidden in a secret room. When they discovered cocaine, they arrested Rubell. Although he was concerned about his friends and the fate of his favorite nightspot, Halston was hurt to learn that all the time he had been bringing friends like Liza to the secret basement room, there was another, more secret room he knew nothing about.

Lost in all the drama behind the scenes at "The Act" was Liza's growing relationship with the stage manager, Mark Gero, the darkly handsome son of Frank Gero.

Frank had been the stage manager of Liza's very first show, "Flora, the Red Menace," but when she asked him to take on the same job for "The Act," he declined because he was co-producing a play of his own. He recommended his son, Mark, a sculptor who had studied anthropology at Connecticut College.

Liza's relationship with Mark survived "The Act," which closed on July 1, 1978. A few weeks later, she traveled to New Brunswick, New Jersey, with him and his brothers to see Frank's play "Are You Now, Or Have You Ever Been?", a drama about the 1950s congressional investigation into Communist activities in the entertainment industry. Soon afterward, Liza took off on her European concert tour.

Early in January 1979 Liza, took her relationship with Mark Gero public when she stepped into his father's show. "Are You Now" had opened in New York in October, and since then, every few weeks, a different celebrated actress, such as Colleen Dewhurst or Tammy Grimes, came in to read the famous letter that Lillian Hellman wrote to the House Un-American Activities Committee.

The devoted Liza coaxed Warhol up to her place at 40 Central Park South to look at Mark's sculpture. Mark wasn't there — he was playing poker with his buddies, and Liza was going to join them later. She asked Warhol to write Mark a note saying how good the stuff was and that he should get Mark a show. "It was tits out of marble and alabaster and wood, and she was rubbing the tits while we talked," Warhol complained.

According to Warhol, Liza's romance with Gero was launched when "he asked her if she wanted to see Paradise, and she said yes, she asked him where it was, and he said in his room, so they went there and fucked."

But Liz Smith jumped the gun a bit January 21, when she informed her readers that Liza planned to announce her engagement to Gero at a Studio 54 party for "Are You Now." Smith was forced to run a rare correction the next day. According to Liza, Smith's "awfully good source" was entirely off the wall. Her divorce from Jack was not even final yet.

Liza considered this a time to stretch and test herself creatively. "I've found that taking left turns is not only good for your sense of self but for your integrity as well," she announced in an interview. "More important, it's given me the courage to do something I've never done, the Covent Garden season with Martha. In July (1979) we're going to do 'Acrobats of the Gods' and 'The Owl and the Pussycat.'"

Liza proved she still had star power when her one-woman show sold out at Carnegie Hall in September. Mark had become her production manger. She was welcomed back with cheers, applause and screams that were reportedly of a magnitude unusual even for her. All her pals were there: Halston, Steve Rubell, Warhol, Diana Vreeland.

Steve even had a party for her at Studio 54. There were three huge candles and a black sequined Halston napkin on every table. Said Vanity Fair's Bob Colacello, "The food was light, but the dish was heavy."

On Nov. 12, 1979, Liza was pregnant and ready to embrace motherhood, although she was not ready to tell the world. She was not even sure she wanted to get married, but Mark convinced her, and on December 4, at 7:15 p.m., Liza, draped in a full-length fur coat, arrived at St. Bartholomew's Episcopal Church on Park Avenue. She slipped inside for the candlelight marriage ceremony that began a few minutes later.

Twenty close friends, including Fred Ebb, Halston and Elizabeth Taylor, and family members including Frank Gero, who was now producing "On Golden

Pond," sat in a half circle at an altar laden with pink and white lilies, roses, lilac and narcissus. The light of about 50 candles was reflected by the church's gold mosaic dome above them.

Liza wore a diaphanous pink chiffon gown designed by Halston, and her maid of honor was her sister Lorna. Mark chose his brothers Jason, 22, and Jonathan, 18. For the third time in 10 years, Vincente gave his daughter away to the man of her dreams. Perhaps he was thinking of one of Liza's Kander and Ebb favorites, "Maybe This Time."

Presiding over the ceremony was the Rev. Peter Delaney, who had married Judy Garland and her fifth and last husband, and months later presided at her funeral. Monsignor Emerson Moore, the Roman Catholic priest for whom Mark had once served as an altar boy, gave a blessing. After organ music and a reading of I Corinthians 13:1-13 — "faith, hope and love, but the greatest of these is love" — the couple exchanged smiles, vows and rings.

Outside on Park Avenue, fans threw rice and yelled, "We love you, Liza!" Liza waved and smiled. Vincente Minnelli said he was "full of wonder." Lorna said she wished Liza "happiness, just happiness." Vincente's longtime companion, Lee Anderson, caught the bride's bouquet. After a black-tie reception at Halston's home on East 63rd Street, the couple left for a honeymoon in Jamaica.

And so Liza was ending a wild and crazy decade, looking forward to a new life with a husband and child. Unfortunately, as was always the case in the life of Liza Minnelli, plans were about to change in a New York minute.

CHAPTER 5

Stepping out

"I have a problem and I'm going to deal with it."

That fall, Liza had teamed with Goldie Hawn to tape the CBS-TV special "Goldie & Liza Together." The two women became friends instantly and they worked so well together that they planned to do the movie version of "Chicago" together.

At 34, Goldie was the mother of 3-year-old Oliver and 10-month-old Kate (the future star of the movie "Almost Famous"). Liza had always loved children, and she became great buddies with Goldie's kids. Goldie was the first person Liza told when she discovered that she was pregnant in November.

According to Halston, Liza had been told that she could not have children, so she was especially surprised and delighted with this news. It was Mark, though, who wanted to get married. He told Liza, "If

we don't get married by the end of the year, that's it."
With two failed marriages behind her, Liza was not so
sure.

"We're living in modern days," she replied. "People
don't necessarily have to get married."

"Yeah, but I want a family, and you want a family,"
he answered. "And I'm not that modern."

On December 10, just a week after her wedding,
Liza was rushed to New York Hospital-Cornell
Medical Center. She was two months pregnant and
feared that she was losing her baby. "She has been
having trouble for more than a week," said a close
friend. "Over the weekend, the pains became
intolerable and she was rushed to the hospital. Liza
was listed in the maternity section under the name of
her manager, Deanna Wemble. Reached at her home,
Wemble confirmed that Liza was in the hospital but
denied it had anything to do with her pregnancy."

Even so, Liza suffered a soon-to-be-publicized
miscarriage.

It's possible that drug abuse contributed to Liza's
problems. Author Wendy Leigh reports that both Liza
and Mark were heavy cocaine users around this time.
According to Leigh, "after 10 years on drugs, Liza
Minnelli was so crazed that she didn't care who saw
her use them — and her cocaine abuse once wrecked
a weekend at the estate of auto tycoon Henry Ford."

Liza and Mark were invited to the magnate's home
at the end of the 1970s. Ford's daughter, who was also
there, later confided to Leigh's source, "It was a
nightmare because Liza and Mark were so coked up
that they didn't make any sense at the dinner table.
They just kept jumping up and going to the

bathroom, being the worst possible houseguests."

"Goldie and Liza Together" aired Feb. 19, 1980. Later in the same year she would be seen on television again, teaming with Misha in his one-hour salute to American musical theater, "Baryshnikov on Broadway." Their romance was long over, but it meant much to Liza that Baryshnikov still valued her talent as a dancer.

"Misha and I talked about working together for years, but that TV special was our first real chance," she said later. "When I think about it now, I realize what an unlikely combination we must have been. I bet lots of people tuned the show in just to see what the hell we were going to do!"

Liza was desperate to try to have another baby. Said her friend Halston, "It's the one thing that Liza wants and needs more than anything, a really strong home and family."

"I know I'm going to get pregnant again soon," Liza said. "When you meet the right guy, you want to have his kid."

She also hoped to make another feature film and told many interviewers that she would gladly put aside her concert schedule for a feature film.

With no studio offers, she tried to develop projects on her own.

In the summer of 1980, Liza was filming a relatively small role in "Arthur," playing Linda Marolla, a drab waitress who shoplifts at Bergdorf-Goodman and catches the eye of Dudley Moore's drunken but loveable millionaire. The effect of 10 years of drinking and drugs showed in Liza's drab face and listless body. Rumors circulated that her alcohol and drug problems had slowed down production.

One member of the production said, "We knew all about the booze and drugs from reliable sources. I felt sorry for her because I don't think she ever grew up, she just acted grown up. She moved into a new home and didn't know how to decorate it. Halston did everything for her; he designed her life, her apartment, her clothes."

Liza and Mark moved into a penthouse on the 21st floor of a modern high-rise in the East 60s. The day they moved in, Mark carried her over the threshold. He asked Halston, who was with them, to leave for a while, because, she explained apologetically, "It was such a personal and private moment."

Liza had envisioned something belle epoque, in the rich, European style of Barbra Streisand's homes, but Halston and the decorator he brought in thought Liza should have a streamlined, modern interior, with room for a nursery.

She celebrated Mark's 30th birthday with a lavish party there, and on Oct. 7, 1980, announced that she was pregnant again. That same week, while appearing in Framingham, Mass., she was rushed to Massachusetts General Hospital, suffering from severe abdominal pains.

The doctors ordered Liza to cancel the rest of her concert season, and she and Mark retreated to the getaway home she'd purchased in Lake Tahoe. There, on New Year's Eve, Liza had her second miscarriage. A spokesperson said, "There is no reason to assume she cannot conceive and have a successful pregnancy."

Determined to go on, Liza returned to her tour on March 16 in Philadelphia. It may have been too soon, though, since on April 22 she was hospitalized at St. Joseph's Infirmary in Atlanta.

"Arthur" was a surprise hit when it opened in July 1981. It was helped along by a memorable theme song, "Best That You Can Do," co-written by Burt Bacharach, Carol Bayer Sager, Peter Allen and Christopher Cross. There were rumors that the film's producers were reluctant to send Liza on publicity tours because of her shaky health. The rumors about her drinking and drug problems probably also hurt her chances to land the roles in big film musicals she so yearned for. She was still hoping to star in "Chicago," but it was years before the stage hit was brought to the screen.

This was not unusual. Paramount Pictures had acquired "Evita" in the summer of 1981 and signed Robert Stigwood to co-produce. The following summer, Liza learned that director Ken Russell, who wanted her for the lead, had been overruled by Stigwood and Paramount. It would take another 15 years for "Evita" to make it to the screen, and when it did, it would be directed by Alan Parker and star Madonna.

It was in the early 1980s that Liza began including some of her mother's songs in her act, something Fred Ebb had been urging her to do for years.

Ebb pointed to the showcase of Liza's awards in her living room: an Oscar, four Tonys and countless others. "It says Liza Minnelli on them, not Judy Garland," he said. "You've arrived. Now we can put some of her songs in your show. Maybe it's time you said thank you."

Liza started with "The Man That Got Away," Judy's

classic from "A Star Is Born." She also performed "The Trolley Song," an upbeat number from "Meet Me in St. Louis," the movie that brought her parents together for the first time.

"In the past, when I'd urge her to do one of Judy's pieces, she'd always say she wasn't ready — either psychologically or as performer," Ebb said in 1984. "Then, one day about two years ago, she just felt she was, and at the end of this number called 'Show-Stoppers,' she made this speech. She said, 'There's one showstopper I left out, and frankly I left it out because I never felt ready to do it before. But I am ready now, and I'd like to sing this showstopping song by a showstopping lady, who was the best friend I ever had.' And then she sang 'The Man That Got Away.' "

On Feb. 28, 1983, Vincente Minnelli would be 80 years old, and Liza, determined that he get all the respect that was his due, helped mount two gala birthday salutes. On February 19, 1983 a retrospective of Vincente's films was held at the Palm Springs Desert Museum. At the museum's Annenberg Theater, she performed for an audience of 450 people, among them Kirk Douglas, Frank and Barbara Sinatra, Gregory and Veronique Peck and Eva Gabor, who had each paid $1,000 a plate. After singing "My Heart Belongs to Daddy," she brought her father up on stage, and in a gentle, sweet voice, he sang to her his favorite song, "Embraceable You."

Vincente's failing health kept him from attending his second birthday party, held in March at New York's Museum of Modern Art. At the last minute he was hospitalized at Cedars-Sinai in Los Angeles, but he sent a telegram that was read aloud to the guests at the Pierre's Cotillion Room.

Liza was joined by friends Lucie Arnaz, Martin Scorsese, Bianca Jagger, Halston, Bill Blass and others for the $500-a-ticket-evening. A joyous Lillian Gish toasted Liza, exclaiming, "You're Vincente's greatest production!"

The party ended with Peter Duchin playing "Happy Birthday" while a huge cake was wheeled into the room. The event raised $100,000 for the museum.

"This is the city my father loved the most," said Liza.

A week later, at the Fairmont Hotel in Dallas, she suffered abdominal cramps and shortness of breath. At 1:30 a.m., Mark called the paramedics, who administered oxygen and convinced a reluctant Liza to admit herself into the hospital. Later her spokesman, Tony Zoppl, insisted that the problem was nothing more than a small piece of steak that lodged in her throat.

However, one biographer noted that "Zoppl's explanation, couched in the language of a circumspect publicist, contained contradictions in that abdominal pain was far more compatible with a possible drug-related anxiety attack than with choking on steak."

Vincente Minnelli had made his mark in New York before he headed to Hollywood for an even more brilliant career. In 1983, another young man, David Gest, was beginning to make his mark in Hollywood, before heading for New York.

A native of Encino, California, Gest grew up with the Jackson Five, and Tito and Michael became his lifelong friends. At age 18, Gest was publicity director for a major record label, and from this he moved on to become one of the town's most prominent personal managers, counting Al Green, The Doobie Brothers, The Captain and Tennille and Burt Bacharach among his clients.

In 1983, already established in the business and looking for a new project, Gest had the idea to create American Cinema Awards. "I thought there was a need for a place where people from all over the world could come to study and learn about the stars and the films — the history of the motion picture industry." There were so many great stars who had never received their due. The foundation could enhance and enlighten the public about their contributions. Gest started by recruiting Joel McCrea, Frances Dee, Joseph Cotton and Patricia Medina as founding patrons.

Liza, meanwhile, was engrossed in her new act, featuring songs from her parents' films. The show was called "By Myself," but Liza still wanted a family and was hoping to get pregnant.

On April 11, 1983, Liza joined Dudley Moore, Richard Pryor and Walter Matthau in co-hosting the Academy Awards and, notably, she chose to wear a Calvin Klein instead of one of Halston's creations.

In an effort to strengthen her marriage, Liza pulled away from the man who was almost everything else in her life: Halston. That summer, Warhol noted that Liza didn't stay at Halston's place in Montauk, on Long Island, and he suspected it was because Liza snubbed Halston at the Academy Awards. He believed that the Gero family was competing with Halston for influence over Liza. He also made the cryptic observation, "I guess Mark knew that Liza was using Halston to have assignations too."

It certainly would have been consistent with Liza's pattern to look for attention from other lovers while sincerely trying to stay with Mark in a failing marriage. She began her affair with Rex Kramer while she was still living with husband Peter Allen, and throughout her marriage to Jack Haley Jr. she had affairs with Martin Scorsese, Mikhail Baryshnikov and Mark.

Liza continued to support her sister, Lorna Luft, as she struggled to establish a career in the shadows of a superstar mother and sister. In July, Liza and Lorna co-hosted a screening of the original uncut version of their mother's film, "A Star Is Born," at Radio City Music Hall.

Liza was also linked to actor Joe Pesci, when they were seen dining together in New Jersey in November. After dinner, Liza sang in the restaurant's piano bar for two hours, but according to Wendy Leigh, when the pianist, a moonlighting plastic surgeon named Hugh Feehan, asked her to sing "You Made Me Love You," Liza declined, saying, "That's my mother's song." In 1983, Pesci was still best known for his role in Scorsese's "Raging Bull." He and Liza both denied a romance, although the rumor persisted.

Liza and Mark celebrated their fourth wedding anniversary with a party at their penthouse in December. Liza wore a red chain mail Halston, and the guests included Martha Graham, Lucille Ball, Chita Rivera, Cher, Al Pacino, Robert De Niro, Bianca Jagger and Charles Aznavour.

She had begun rehearsals for her return to Broadway in "The Rink," a musical drama by Terrence McNally with music and lyrics by Kander and Ebb. The show reunited Liza and Chita and included future "Seinfeld" star Jason Alexander. Liza played a secondary role: the headstrong daughter coming to terms with her spirited mother, played by Chita.

During rehearsal, Liza decided to stop drinking for a week. "I'd done that many times before for even longer periods," she later said. "This time I only got through four days." It was a warning signal.

"The Rink" opened at the Martin Beck Theater on Feb. 9, 1984. Once again, Liza could not escape Judy's legend. Her role required her to delve into her own memories of growing up and separating from her mother. She didn't realize how painful this process would be until it was too late.

In March, just in time for Liza's 38th birthday, PBS ran six programs devoted to Judy Garland. They included footage of Liza's first appearances on Judy's CBS show in 1963. When Liza talked about her mother and their relationship, she claimed that her mother's death almost 15 years earlier had actually brought them closer together. "Back then, I'd have to go through long-distance operators and all that to get to where she was — on a boat or someplace — just to call to tell her something funny that I'd read . . . Mama's death took that away, because now I just look up and ask." The interview ended on a poignant note with Liza's comment that if she ever had a daughter, she would name her Judy.

Liza and Chita were nominated for Tony Awards as best actress in a musical for their performances in "The Rink." Chita won, and in the excitement of the moment at the ceremony, forgot to thank Liza in her acceptance speech. She thanked everyone else, and it immediately set tongues wagging before Chita had even left the stage and realized what she had done. Later she insisted it was an oversight, and apologized profusely and repeatedly. "I could never have done the show without this wonderful woman," Chita insisted.

Liza's health had been deteriorating through the brief run of "The Rink" and it worsened after the Tony Awards. In July she missed six shows after she was reportedly injured in a taxi accident. Other members of the cast noticed that she didn't sound any better when she came back. She had always been the kind of person who could perform until late at night and still bound out of bed early in the morning.

Although Liza didn't know it until later, all the Valium she was taking was building up in her system and combining with the alcohol for a disastrous effect. She began sleeping in, and after a morning cup of coffee, she'd opt for a nap. That would kill more hours, and then she would stare at television soap operas for hours. Finally, she was staying in bed all day. "I'd force myself up at 6:30 and into gear to do the show," she said, "I got weaker and weaker." Liza was convinced she had mononucleosis or hypoglycemia. She saw two doctors, but neither of them found anything wrong with her, and both prescribed Valium.

Liza's personal life was also deteriorating. Whereas once she and Mark had been inseparable, as the pressures around "The Rink" took their toll, Liza grew distant and uncommunicative, especially with Mark. She was soon suggesting that they separate.

Lorna later described Liza's collapse in her memoir, "Me and My Shadows." According to her sister, Liza was often so unhappy while appearing in "The Rink" that she would show up at Lorna's apartment after a performance and spend the night on her couch rather than go home to Mark. With a husband and new baby, Lorna's life now had the stability that Liza's lacked. Liza was short-tempered and often erupted in anger, then tears. The cast of "The Rink" put up with her nightly temper tantrums, but by July 11, she had missed 14 performances, and Lorna knew that "Liza was in trouble."

That night, after a late dinner with Barry Landau, Liza complained about pain in her neck. Landau took her to Beth Israel Hospital, where doctors immediately removed a mole on her back and prepared for a routine biopsy.

"Liza panicked at the word biopsy," Landau later said. She was convinced that she had cancer and grew more anxious. Another friend blamed this on "drug jitters. She was acting paranoid."

Fearful for Liza's condition, her personal assistant, Roni Agress, called Lorna from the hospital and said, "I need help." Lorna left her 4-month-old son with a friend and raced to Liza's bedside. Liza's friend and publicist, Allen Eichhorn, was also on the scene, but Lorna was distressed to see that Landau was already whispering on a pay phone. She was convinced he was leaking the story to a gossip columnist.

Lorna soon learned that although Liza did not have cancer, the doctors at Beth Israel were so concerned about her condition that they wanted to admit her for a psychiatric evaluation. Recognizing that this could be disastrous, Lorna moved quickly. For the next 72 hours, while her friend Arlene Lazar looked after her son, Lorna battled to save her sister's life and keep the story from the press. She refused to allow the psychiatric evaluation and moved Liza to New York Hospital. They, too, insisted on a psychiatric evaluation and told Lorna that if she refused, she would "have to have her [sister] admitted to a psychiatric ward or a locked ward." Liza was admitted under an assumed name.

Lorna knew that Elizabeth Taylor was currently at the Betty Ford Center. She contacted Elizabeth's longtime personal assistant and gatekeeper, Chen Sam, for the name of Elizabeth's doctor. Sam referred Lorna to Dr. Bill Skinner, who gave her valuable guidance for dealing with Liza's condition. Next, Lorna contacted her godfather, Frank Sinatra, who put his private plane at Liza's disposal, no questions asked.

Meanwhile, Roni and Allen scrambled to handle the press for Liza and the show. She was not going to return to "The Rink," and an understudy would have to replace her immediately.

Lorna and Roni were not the only ones worried about Liza. Pam Reinhardt Lewis, a childhood friend from Liza's Beverly Hills days, was staying at Liza's apartment, came to the hospital to tend to Liza while Lorna made arrangements to get her sister admitted to the Betty Ford Center in Rancho Mirage, 15 miles outside of Palm Springs. They agreed not to tell Liza what was happening yet. With Dr. Skinner, Lorna, Roni and Pam planned an intervention.

Things were still touch and go, with Liza resisting the idea that she had a problem, until she happened to catch a TV news clip that showed Elizabeth Taylor leaving the Betty Ford Center that very day. She looked and sounded so good that Liza decided — on her own — that it might work for her, too.

On July 13, 1984, Liza entered the Betty Ford Center. With characteristic enthusiasm, she embraced the routine. She woke up at 6:30 a.m. with the other patients; made her own bed; and, after breakfast in the cafeteria, she participated in meditation, exercise classes, therapy and alcohol counseling. In the beginning her visitors were limited to Lorna, friend Patty Lewis, Elizabeth Taylor and her stepfather, Sid Luft.

Stockard Channing stepped into Liza's role in "The Rink," but it was not enough to save the show, which closed August 4 after 204 performances.

At first, the official story was that Liza had a bad reaction to anesthesia during surgery for removal of the cyst. When news leaked that she was actually at the Betty Ford Center, she issued a statement: "I have a problem and I'm going to deal with it." Comparisons to Judy's problems with alcohol and pills were irresistible and frequently made.

Mark barely made an appearance in the initial stories about Liza's problems. Friends still denied any trouble in the marriage and dismissed rumors to this effect as "absolutely untrue."

A radiant and rejuvenated Liza left the Betty Ford Center in September. She believed that her problems had started with the Valium doctors prescribed during her mother's funeral. In an article in People, she said, "In the following years I developed a whole new soothing vocabulary: Valium, Librium, Dalmane, all nice sounding names." She also drank, she admitted, adding, "when I drank, I drank silly little drinks with silly sounding names at first. I tried hard liquor, and eventually settled on wine."

She seemed to dance around the issue of hard drug use, saying, "They are easy to take, a line of cocaine at a party or something like that. I'm too hyper as it is, so who needed help? I hate marijuana, prefer champagne and my tolerance is immense." She stressed that she had never taken anything to go on stage to work, but she would have a drink immediately after a performance.

She also said that the separation from Mark had lasted only four days and that "he came to me immediately." He even took Liza and Lorna to the airport. He wanted to go with them, but, according to Liza, the Betty Ford Center advised against it.

When she was ready for Family Week, Mark joined her. They were both committed to their marriage. "Nothing deterred him from making our life together work," Liza said. "And it has. Our marriage is fine. We understand each other and accept each other's faults." Liza concluded by saying that she wanted to get back to movies and to television. "I'm going to live in California for a while now and work on film projects. Mark is sculpting and has a show coming up in Los Angeles, so he'll be working here, too."

Liza returned to New York at the beginning of 1985. She was in high spirits, and even her marriage seemed stronger. She and Mark were seen holding hands at a tennis tournament at Madison Square Garden in February.

Liza was not out of the woods yet, however, just weeks later, she suddenly dropped from sight and rumors circulated that she was back in rehab. On

March 1, her publicist, Allen Eichhorn, confirmed that Liza "wanted to get away from that [Hollywood] to concentrate on reinforcing the success that she had." Liza had not "fallen off the wagon," he insisted, but just needed reinforcement. He declined to reveal where she was staying, but it soon came out that Liza had checked into the Hazelden Clinic in Minnesota. She was to kick off a concert tour in May and wanted to be in the best possible condition.

In November, Liza told her friend Maxine Mesinger that she was working with Stevie Phillips on a feature film "about an alcoholic lady who licks her problem." The project was not autobiographical, she assured Mesinger. "My alcohol and drug problem was too dull to make into a movie," she said. "I did not have enough real problems to make it interesting." Phillips had been Liza's first agent way back when she was apprenticing at Hyannisport summer theater and had gone on to produce the long-running Broadway musical "The Best Little Whorehouse in Texas."

Liza took time out for what she called her first dramatic role, the lead in a television movie called "A Time to Live," which was based on "Intensive Care," a memoir by Marylou Weisman about her son's struggle with muscular dystrophy. Liza eventually won a Golden Globe for her work in the movie, yet this did not seem to interest directors casting films.

Liza seemed to be on a never-ending concert tour, but she believed taking three months off twice a year left plenty of time for a film. She was happy that Mark had given up drinking, too. "We both feel wonderful," said Liza. "It's so great getting up in the morning and feeling really good."

On March 12, 1986, Liza celebrated her 40th birthday with concert performances at the Palladium in
London that would be televised on HBO. During the
concert, Liza joked, "All kinds of wonderful
people keep telling me that life begins at 40 — it
seems like I breathed easier at 23."

Some critics were disappointed that she was no
longer the perky, fresh-faced Liza with a Z. Gwen
Verdon danced into her 50s and so did Chita, but Liza
seemed to be wearing out.

"I'm strong, I'm happy," she insisted in the concert.

In April 1986, Liza teamed up with Frank Sinatra
for the first time at the Golden Nugget in Atlantic
City. There was some discussion about who would
sing "New York, New York." After all, the song had
been written for Liza and had become her virtual
anthem. Since then, however, Sinatra had recorded it
and it had become one of his biggest hits. Liza and
Frank agreed to skip the song in their separate acts and
then unite at the end for a medley of New York songs,
including "New York, New York."

While Liza struggled with her health, young David
Gest was in Hollywood, marking the 3rd anniversary
of the American Cinema Awards, which he had built
into a local institution.

At 31, Gest was making a name for himself in the
tight-knit Hollywood entertainment community. In a
May 30 profile in the Los Angeles Times, John Voland
wrote, "Even set against a landscape blurry with Big
Thinkers, David Gest stands out." His 1985
American Cinema Awards, with co-hosts Elizabeth
Taylor, Robert Wagner and Robert Mitchum, were
becoming known as events to be seen at, and his

foundation had acquired almost nine acres of prime beachfront property in Malibu for a future film center.

The June American Cinema Awards Foundation dinner at the Beverly Wilshire brought out Dick Van Dyke, Janet Leigh, Ann-Margret and Bobby Rydell to reprise numbers from "Bye Bye Birdie" — the very show that made Liza fall in love with musicals when she was 13 years old.

On July 4, Liza was part of the celebration at the Statue of Liberty, and Gregory Peck would later describe her performance as "perfection" and, for him, the high point of the event.

In late July, Liza managed to spend two days with her ailing father before heading for Monte Carlo. Vincente had been in and out of Cedars-Sinai Medical Center for the last year, suffering from emphysema and pneumonia. On July 25, she was getting off a plane in Paris when she was told that her father had died in his sleep. He was 83. She immediately turned around and headed back to Los Angeles.

A small group of about 100 mourners gathered for the funeral at the Wee Kirk o' the Heather at Forest Lawn Memorial Park in Glendale. Michael Jackson escorted Liza and the widow, Lee Anderson. Mark was there, as was Vincente's other daughter, Christiana Nina, but they made it into few stories or photographs. Gregory Peck and Kirk Douglas delivered the eulogies. Peck recalled working with Lauren Bacall in Minnelli's "Designing Women," a sophisticated comedy, in 1957. "He'd shout out just before every scene, with that big grin of his, 'All right, folks, light up your noses!' And it was perfect direction."

Of all his memories of Vincente, Douglas said, the one he most treasured was Liza's tribute to her father on the stage of the Palm Springs Museum, when she brought Vincente up on stage, and he sang to her his favorite song, "Embraceable You."

During the 30-minute service, Peck read condolences from President and Mrs. Reagan and the French Minister of Culture. Father George O'Brien, a Catholic priest with the Church of the Good Shepherd in Beverly Hills, gave a blessing. Jack Haley Jr., James Stewart, Ricardo Montalban, Kirk Douglas, Kenny Rogers, Henry Mancini and Fred de Cordova were pallbearers.

Vincente's will, filed in Los Angeles Superior Court on July 31, had a few surprises. For one thing, he had specified that he should be cremated and there be no funeral. These directions had been disregarded and instead, there was a Roman Catholic service at the Wee Kirk and he was buried at Forest Lawn. It's impossible to believe that Liza would have intentionally ignored her father's wishes, and it must have distressed her to learn that she had given him a beautiful service that he did not want. Vincente left $100,000 to Lee, but only $5,000 to Christiana Nina. She was now married with two small children, Vincent and Ximena, and Vincente said in the will that he knew she was already well provided for. He left the Beverly Hills mansion to Liza, but requested that Lee be permitted to continue living there.

At the end of 1986, Liza began to move on, spending New Year's Eve with Mark and his parents in London, and then she headed for Rome for a reunion with Burt Reynolds. Liza and Mark joined Burt and Loni

Anderson for a cruise down Florida's Intracoastal Waterway. Liza and Burt had both fallen far since the glory days when they were filming "Lucky Lady" in Mexico. In her memoir "My Life in High Heels," Anderson recalled that Burt was "cantankerous the entire trip." Liza told her, "I love him like a brother, but I don't know how you can stand it."

As she took the stage at Carnegie Hall May 28 for a three-week run, Liza looked like she was winning her struggle with alcohol and drugs. Midway through her two-hour performance, she told the audience, "Lots of people say things can't change. I'm here to tell you they're wrong." Mark was in the audience, singing along with the finale of "New York, New York" and at her side during the party that followed. A radiant Liza assured the guests "Work agrees with me."

Nothing validated Liza's commitment to sobriety more than her new adventure with Estee Lauder. Celebrity fragrances were a major marketing story in 1987. Elizabeth Taylor's Passion, launched that year, was one of the 10 most popular scents, and consumers were expected to shell out $50 million for her essence in 1988.

Leonard Lauder was looking for a big idea to launch Estee Lauder's new men's fragrance, Metropolis. He wanted a big personality, someone who would personify all the glamour of the big city. He found it in Liza. Alvin Chereskin, a Lauder executive, described the talent hunt: "We thought Liza epitomized the big city singer. Like Edith Piaf represented Paris, we thought Liza was New York."

In September, Lauder for Men announced that Liza Minnelli would become the spokeswoman for their new men's fragrance. They lavished her with attention, hosting a luncheon for her at the Four Seasons, and Liza began with personal appearances in New York at Bloomingdale's and Macy's.

Liza filmed her first ever commercial for a product, a glamorous 30-second spot for Metropolis. While singing "City Lights" from "The Act," Liza smiled and danced around New York City nightspots in a short, low-cut, beaded Bob Mackie dress. There was Liza at the Plaza, at a theater in Chelsea, at a flower market, at the Empire Diner and in the middle of traffic at Columbus Circle. In the last shot, Liza stood on a promenade of the Brooklyn Bridge, kissing a handsome man — Mark Gero. Liza had refused to do the shot with anyone but her husband.

The production team loved working with Liza. "She's a big star but she's a pussycat," Chereskin added. "She's the least difficult person you ever worked with."

The only near-disaster came when Liza's wardrobe from Bob Mackie arrived from California. The production team had discovered that everything Liza wore had big patch pockets. She liked to keep things like her cigarettes in them, and they also gave her something to do with her hands. According to ad agency executive Linda Becker, "The wardrobe arrived one day before the shoot and lo and behold, there were no pockets on her dress. We called California and had the pockets flown in by Federal Express and sewn on at the last minute."

Fred Ebb wrote some new lyrics for "City Lights," and Liza spent an entire day in the recording studio with a 30-piece orchestra and her musical director Bill

Lavorgna redoing the song. Liza could not wait around for the mixing, however. She was on her way to Paris to begin a new world tour. Becker sent her a tape, and Liza asked them to make the horns hotter, so they remixed the music, which she finally approved. The tag line was: "Metropolis — Live in it and you own the world!"

Metropolis soon accounted for 36 percent of Estee Lauder's total sales in Bloomingdale's New York store alone. The store's cosmetics buyer considered it "the best men's launch we've ever done."

After a seven-year hiatus (except for cameos in Scorsese's "The King of Comedy" in 1983 and "The Muppets Take Manhattan" in 1984), Liza now had two major films coming out in 1988, "Rent-a-Cop" and "Arthur 2: On the Rocks."

At the 1988 Academy Awards, Liza and Dudley Moore presented the Oscar for best song and sang a duet. Liza's friend Sally Kirkland had been nominated for her role in "Anna," and Liza gave her a butterfly pin for good luck. Mark, increasingly absent from Liza's public appearances, did not attend. After the ceremony, Liza made the Oscar night party rounds with sister Lorna. She lingered with her in Los Angeles, and they had a girls' night out with old friends Lucie Arnaz, Ann Turkel and Jackie Collins.

Liza's next project brought her back to New York, where in April she began filming an ambitious television special. "Triple Play" was filmed in the city on a 10-day schedule and would air on ABC. It consisted of three unrelated one-act plays by Terrence McNally, Lanford Wilson, Wendy Wasserstein and Kander and Ebb. Liza played three totally different women.

"It was like working on three characters at once," she said. "We gave the writers of the separate segments four lines only, and told them to write a story around them. No one knew what the other was doing, and it's fabulous."

In the first segment she played a junkie, and Ryan O'Neal was her pimp. In the second she ran away to Africa with Louis Gossett Jr. The third teamed her with John Rubinstein.

Liza had also agreed to replace an ailing Dean Martin on tour with Frank and Sammy. She would join them September 17 at the Summit in Houston.

As part of her Metropolis deal, Liza had agreed to promote the fragrance with personal appearances in select stores. Estee Lauder treated her like a star, sending hundreds of red carnations (Liza's favorite flower) to her hotel suite in Houston where she appeared at two Foley's department stores. Three thousand people stood in line just to meet her. A local reporter asked her why she was promoting a men's fragrance, and Liza answered, "because I'd rather smell a man than a woman."

Liza's stop in Houston was part of a four-day, four-city personal appearance tour to Los Angeles, Chicago, Houston and Dallas. Liza was enthusiastic, telling reporters that Metropolis "is part of a ritual of getting dressed. It's part of the dating game. My husband wears it. So do I. So do a lot of my friends. I don't think I've ever given it to anyone who hasn't worn it."

Liza confessed that she had no idea why Lauder named the fragrance Metropolis. "Most cities are so dirty and this seems like a very clean fragrance to me.

I think probably if you smell clean, it helps you out through the day."

She had also adopted a new puppy, a cairn terrier she named Lilli. "She looks just like Toto, Mama's dog in 'The Wizard of Oz,' and she's wonderful," said Liza. "Mark would never let me have a dog before."

Liza began a one-month break May 16. She had not had a day off in so long that she was nervous about what she would do. She planned to spend two weeks seeing friends in New York, after which she and Mark would take a two-week cruise to the South of France with Leslie Bricusses and George Hamilton.

Liza had not seen the rough cut for "Arthur 2: On the Rocks," but the word was good. In the movie, Liza returned to the role of Linda Marolla, now happily married to Arthur. The character was the kind of girl who goes straight ahead, one step at a time, and deals with the days as they come along. But was the drunken playboy Arthur still as funny in the 1980s?

Liza hit Hollywood again in July on a whirlwind promotional tour for "Arthur 2: On the Rocks." She had been busy going through her father's films to prepare for a PBS special, "Minnelli on Minnelli." The process ignited a desire to do more films.

"As I started to look at his work," Liza explained, "it struck me how incredible film is, how lasting. Having done so much work that you do one night and then it's gone, I felt I'd really like to concentrate on film for now, maybe let it stay there for a minute. My film career is not really as spotty as many people seem to think it is. I really haven't made that many pictures." In fact, she had made only 10 pictures in two decades. She insisted that the limited output was her choice.

"Movies are an art form that you have to devote time to," she continued. "I've never been one to be able to slip them in in-between. And then, it's not exactly like I've been sitting on a bench for the past few years."

Liza was ready now to commit the time to a film, and she looked forward to the collaborative effort. "You're so isolated when you're out doing concerts," she explained. "The best thing about it is not having to perform alone anymore, not going out there, pouring out your heart singing your songs and then going home alone."

When "Arthur 2: On the Rocks" opened, Liza and Dudley discovered how much times had changed. Moviegoers were not as amused by a lovable drunk anymore, and Liza's character was regarded as an enabler. She told interviewers that she had thought about that, but decided that "the character of the millionaire playboy lovable drunk is a classic American character. It was not reality but fantasy, like 'My Man Godfrey.' No, it didn't bother me at all because, as I said, this is a classic kind of film. It's got its own message without preaching. I think that it says all the right stuff for this day and age. You've got to take responsibility. You've got to grow up."

No sooner had Liza been talking about committing to more films than she was relieved to hit the concert tour again. Joining Frank Sinatra and Sammy Davis in Houston, she said, "Sometimes I'm on the stage and I think, 'Gee, that's Frank Sinatra. And that's Sammy Davis. If I'm this excited about working with them, imagine what the audience must be feeling watching them. There's so much love between us on that stage, it has to rub off on the audience."

Sammy added, "Frank left everything up to Liza and me for the portion we're all onstage together. We wanted to give the best of Frank, Liza and me, and we did it with such love and affection."

When interviewers asked about her rarely seen husband, Liza's standard response was that Mark was building them a log cabin in upstate New York, and between that and his work in his studio, he was unable to join her on the road. Her constant companion was Lilli, who waited for her in her dressing room night after night.

While singing with Sinatra and Davis, Liza had also been exploring new music styles. She had met Gene Simmons of KISS at Halston's in 1979, when he was involved in a heavy relationship with Cher. Since then they had become good friends, and whenever Simmons was in New York they would get together. In his memoir, "Kiss and Makeup," Simmons insists that he had no romantic aspirations and was not even interested in getting into the Liza Minnelli business.

But whenever they did get together, they talked about music. Liza wanted to know all about KISS. She wanted to know how the band had gone from obscurity to worldwide fame. Simmons explained that it wasn't a matter of one person. "It was a huge confluence of record labels and management," he said.

What really bothered Liza was Madonna's success. By 1987, Madonna seemed to be everywhere.

"She said there was nothing that Madonna had that she didn't have, except for the right songs," Simmons recalled. He told Liza that her "Ethel Merman style of singing" was old-fashioned. "The average teenage girl didn't know a thing about that world. If she was interested in letting go of her past and re-creating Liza Minnelli, then I could help her out. I became her business manager."

As Simmons became more involved in Liza's career, they were seen and photographed everywhere. He insists their relationship was totally professional. "I would meet with her at her apartment and then we would meet at the Fifth Avenue penthouse where I lived. We talked endlessly about movies, music and her aspirations to break into the pop field. I enjoyed her company. I enjoyed going to events with her, like the grand opening of the first Hard Rock Cafe. I respected her as an artist, and I wanted to help her with her career. But that was all I wanted."

Simmons brought Liza to Columbia Records and introduced her to another legend: Walter Yetnikoff. "He gave us the green light right away. He didn't waste time looking at bottom lines or consulting with vice presidents. He was a classic mogul," Simmons explained. "A young A&R guy named Michael Goldstone came up with an idea to put Liza with the Pet Shop Boys and do a modern Euro-disco album. I explained this to Liza and told her what it would require."

Liza liked the Pet Shop Boys' offbeat style of dance music with a tough edge. She liked the biting, cynical quality of their songs and their dramatic quality, too. She thought she could fit their style easily. If she was going to do a pop album, she might as well go all the way — as far away from her image as possible.

Liza had first met with the Pet Shop Boys in July 1987. They wanted to find out if they could work with her. "We were nervous, of course, meeting this superstar," said Neil Tennant. "We wanted to like her because we wanted to work with her. If she had been one of those stars with a big ego and told us, 'I won't do this or this or this,' well, we couldn't have worked with her. But we all got along right away. That was the giant step. She wanted to put herself in our hands. Well, who could resist that?"

The Pet Shop Boys were supposed to just do a few cuts on the album, but after they met Liza and started discussing ideas, she wanted them to do the whole album. One of their suggestions was Tanita Tikaram's "Twist in My Sobriety." "We wanted her to do 'Sobriety' as this outrageous, psychotic song, but weren't sure she'd go for it," Tennant recalled. "Everybody knows about Liza and drug rehab and all that. But she got a big kick out of doing a song that mentioned sobriety."

The album, titled "Results," was released in late September 1989 and included the songs "Losing My Mind," "Twist in My Sobriety" and two Pet Shop Boys covers, "Rent" and "Tonight Is Forever."

"Losing My Mind," released as a single, was a huge hit everywhere except in the United States. It went to number one in England.

"I feel the need to take risks now," Liza told an interviewer. "Maybe it's my age, or those publicized changes in my life, or maybe it's something bizarre, like the position of the planets — who knows? I just know I was driven to do something different — like this album."

She acknowledged that some people might wonder why she was doing "dance music stuff. But where is it written that Liza Minnelli can't sing dance music — or anything she feels like?"

The reporter reminded Liza that she was mostly regarded as an easy-listening performer — and not at all hip. "But I am hip," Liza protested. "I like Heavy D and Joan Jett. I listen to a lot of current music. What I'm about musically isn't just what I sing with Frank and Sammy."

The Pet Shop Boys were not surprised that "Results" had a better reception in Europe. "She has a different stature in Europe," they said. "She's a colossal star, she's treated with reverence. In America, Liza is perceived as this Vegas performer. That's a stigma in America, but not in Europe. Europeans love the Vegas glitter and Liza projects that.

"In Europe this album was an event," said Tennant. "In America, she has to struggle to get radio play. It's very weird when you're treated better in foreign countries than you are in your home country. That can't make her feel very good."

When Simmons decided to start his own record company, he and Liza parted company. "She wanted to go back full into the high-stepping and belting tradition of singing. I wasn't in favor of it; I thought people would think she was just putting on a mask as a modern pop singer. She couldn't break free of Broadway. To some people, that may have been important stuff. To the record-buying public, it meant nothing. In the end we couldn't make it work." Simmons met with Liza's attorney, Mickey Rudin, and dissolved their agreement.

An era ended with the passing of Steve Rubell on July 26, 1989. Life had certainly been a lot quieter since the feds closed down Studio 54 and charged Steve and his partner, Ian Schrager, with tax evasion. Since serving three and a half years in prison for tax evasion, both men had put their energy into the hotel business and another club, Palladium. The cause of death was announced as complications from hepatitis and septic shock but was widely believed to be AIDS.

CHAPTER 6

Love and loss

"I'm a good girl now."

The 1990s brought struggle and sadness for Liza. She was fighting to stay sober and to jump-start her once promising film career, and as AIDS swept through the entertainment community, she experienced the loss of many close friends.

Some women might find consolation in their marriage and family, but Liza was getting little emotional support from her third husband, Mark Gero. He was rarely at her side during the many public appearances that were part of her job. Liza clung to the marriage mainly because she still hoped to have a child. In fact, she was so desperate to conceive after two miscarriages that she secretly visited the famed Omega Institute of Health in New Orleans.

Founded by fertility specialist Dr. Joseph Bellina in 1974, the institute has pioneered gynecological surgery that enables women to conceive and attracts patients from all over the world. After undergoing surgery at the institute and becoming pregnant, Liza suffered a third miscarriage.

In 1988, secretly suffering from AIDS, Halston had sold his beloved New York townhouse and retreated to a secluded penthouse at the Mark Hopkins Hotel in San Francisco. At the beginning of 1990, he checked out and moved to Santa Rosa to spend his final days with his sister. Although Liza no longer visited, she telephoned him regularly. On March 26, Roy Halston Frowick died in his sleep at Pacific Presbyterian Medical Center. Halston's family held a service at San Francisco's Calvary Presbyterian Church. Liza attended, her face almost hidden by huge dark sunglasses, and later joined other mourners at a small reception.

Liza believed that she never got to say goodbye to Halston properly. She opened up about the loss in a 1996 interview. "When he died, I thought — What am I going to do without this person? He was my family! He was my brother. He protected me. He kept me away from everything. He kept me away from . . ." Liza paused, and the interviewer jokingly suggested, "Drugs?" That brought a laugh from Liza.

By that time, thanks to the "Warhol Diaries," published in 1989, it was well known that Halston had supplied Liza with drugs while she was juggling affairs with Baryshnikov and Scorsese in the wild, wild 1970s. By now, Liza was struggling to stay sober, but she was too loyal to ever blame her drug problems on her old friend, especially now that he was lost to her forever. She protected his reputation the same way she struggled to protect her mother's.

Even so, stories about Liza's odd or erratic behavior piled up in the next few years. In one incident, Liza stunned a handsome young fan at a Vegas restaurant when he gave her roses and asked for a keepsake. She slipped off to the ladies' room, then returned and handed him her red bra. Liza, Madonna and other celebrities were spotted at Manhattan's Edelweiss Club, which catered to straight businessmen who liked to relax after work by slipping into cocktail dresses, wigs and makeup for a little dancing with other cross-dressers and transvestites.

With her friends dying off and her marriage to Mark in trouble, Liza found some happiness in indulging her cairn terrier Lilli. She spent hundreds of dollars a week calling Lilli twice a day from wherever she was. Lilli's "nanny" would hold the phone to Lilli's ear. Liza did most of the talking.

Meanwhile, her pal, Sammy Davis Jr., was losing his battle with throat cancer and was sent home from the hospital. Liza arrived at his doorstep, moving in for several days to comfort the old friend who had taught her his tap steps. The Sunday afternoon sing-alongs at his house that she'd loved as a child were long since over, but Fred Ebb would immortalize them in a song, "Sundays at Sammy's."

Sammy died May 16, 1990 and it seemed as if everyone in the business turned out for his funeral service at Forest Lawn in Burbank — Sammy had left instructions that nobody should be turned away. The facility seated 1,500 mourners, and loudspeakers were set up for another 5,000 outside. Liza sat in the first row with Sammy's widow, Altovise, and Barbara and

Frank Sinatra and their daughters, Tina and Nancy. A priest and a rabbi conducted the service, Jesse Jackson delivered a eulogy, and Michael Jackson even contributed a few words. Funeral directors said that the procession to the interment was the longest they had ever seen.

In July 1990, after Liza spent 45 minutes serenading an audience with songs from her father's films, she tilted her face heavenward and wished him a happy Father's Day. The tribute was part of a gala opening for "Directed by Vincente Minnelli," an eight-week retrospective at the Los Angeles County Museum. Some 600 guests gathered at the museum to pay homage to films such as "An American in Paris" and "Gigi." This may have been the inspiration for the "Minnelli on Minnelli" project that Liza would work on for the next 10 years.

On a happier note, Liza became an aunt for the second time on September 21, 1990, when Lorna gave birth to Vanessa Jade Hooker at Cedars-Sinai, the same hospital where Liza had come into the world 44 years earlier.

As the year moved to a close, Mark finally moved out of the apartment on East 69th Street. Liza tried to be upbeat about their separation when she ran into columnist Liz Smith later at a party for Frank Sinatra's 75th birthday. "She was glowing and crowing, having a wonderful time," Smith reported. Liza assured her that the separation was a mutual decision. That was all they wanted to say.

Liza was with Lorna, who was appearing at the Rainbow & Stars cabaret at Rockefeller Center. Liza and Lorna spent most of their time with Liz Smith raving about 3-month-old Vanessa Jade. Lorna said, "She may be my child, but she is just Liza all over again. She looks like Liza, behaves like Liza."

Liza rang in 1991 in Paris with her old friend Charles Aznavour and his family and friends and started planning a new tour with him. Now that she had found the strength to leave another marriage, Liza was ready to try new things both personally and professionally. She was preparing a new show, "Stepping Out," that she promised would be fun.

Liza took a break from rehearsals for "Stepping Out" to celebrate her 45th birthday with the Rockettes. Surrounded by the dancers, Liza looked happy but tired as she cut into her birthday cake. She opened "Stepping Out" at Radio City Music Hall not long afterward, and she played to a packed house in the 6,000-seat theater every night. The three-week engagement was extended another couple weeks, and the Music Hall asked her to bring it back later that year.

The stage show "Stepping Out" was completely different from the film of the same name that Liza released later in 1991. Liza's choreographer for the stage show was Susan Stroman, who was assisted by another old friend, Lisa Mordante, daughter of Chita Rivera. The chorus line was unusual: all women, ages 16 to 60. The stage show also had elements that would eventually bring Liza back to Broadway with "Minnelli on Minnelli."

Liza had only recently discovered her father's early history with the fabled Radio City Music Hall. When she learned that Vincente had been a production designer there in the 1930s, before he went to

Hollywood, she asked to see some of the old photographs of his work from that era.

During the engagement at Radio City, she flashed those Garland legs as she posed outside the Music Hall on Sixth Avenue, which had been temporarily renamed "Minnelli Way" in honor of her appearance.

In "Stepping Out" the movie, filmed mostly in Toronto, Liza played a former Broadway dancer who was struggling to run a tap dance school in a church basement.

"There's a lot of 'A Chorus Line' in it," Liza admitted, but she really loved that it was about "ordinary people." Liza thought it was a good mix of music, comedy and drama. Among the outstanding actors cast along with Liza were Jane Krakowski (of "Ally McBeal" fame), Shelley Winters, Ellen Greene and Bill Irwin.

Everyone wanted the movie to work for Liza's sake. Even Kay Thompson, now 90-something, made a rare public appearance at a screening. When the film opened Sept. 30, 1991, Roger Ebert of the Chicago Sun-Times called it "an amateur-night version of 'A Chorus Line.' Still, the production numbers featuring Liza left him "wishing for more Liza and fewer problems with the chorus." He lamented the fact that nobody made the kind of movies that showed Liza's talents to advantage anymore. "It's a shame that a talent like hers has to survive in an era when the traditional film musical is all but dead." Unfortunately, Liza was "stuck in scenes of potted dialogue and motion where she's chain-smoking and sympathizing."

Although Rex Reed dubbed "Stepping Out" "the feel-good movie of the year," the film was caught in a power shift at Paramount and never got the marketing support it deserved.

Although Mark had moved out in November 1990, Liza still hoped she could save their marriage. In February, she had made a touching last-ditch effort to reconcile with him, and they had begun seeing a New York marriage counselor twice a week. Unfortunately, it was too little, too late.

Liza had a new man in her life, Billy Stritch, who shared her love of music and nightlife. Born in Sugarland, Texas, the lanky pianist and singer arrived in New York as part of a jazz vocal trio, Montgomery, Plant and Stritch, that performed at small clubs such as Don't Tell Mama as well as chic boites at the Algonquin and the Carlyle. When the trio broke up in 1990, Montgomery and Plant went home to Texas, but Stritch stayed on in Manhattan, playing piano two nights a week at Bobo's, a club in the theater district. One night in 1991, Liza Minnelli walked in and his life changed forever.

In an interview, Liza talked about her romance with Stritch, who was 27, and her desire to bear a child. "The truth is, I fell in love with Billy and I can't hide it. With Billy, I think I have found happiness. My happiness would be much bigger if only one day I could be a mother. I haven't lost hope."

Liza was still desperate to become a mother. Although she had always been an adoring aunt to Lorna's two children, Jesse and Vanessa, she told a friend, "Being an auntie is great, but I would trade almost anything in the world to hear some little person call me mom."

At 45, Liza knew that her chances for motherhood were slim, but in the summer of 1991 she made a desperate last-ditch effort to get pregnant. On August 23, she and Billy underwent tests at the famed Omega Institute of Health in New Orleans, La. Observers noted that Liza's nails were bitten "practically to the cuticles." She introduced Stritch as an entertainer friend from Texas, but she confided to one of the medical assistants, "This is the father of my soon-to-be child."

If the tests confirmed that Liza could conceive, she would return to the clinic and be monitored closely to determine the best time and conditions for conception. Although Liza's divorce from Mark Gero was not yet final, she was determined to have Billy's baby as soon as possible. The two started wearing matching platinum friendship rings.

While trying to get pregnant, Liza struggled valiantly to maintain her sobriety even as she was mourning the deaths of Halston and Sammy Davis Jr. She threw herself into AIDS fund-raisers and visiting the sick, and she returned to Radio City Music Hall in early 1992 with a revised version of "Stepping Out" that was taped for television.

Peter never did tell Liza how seriously ill he was, not even when he came back to New York in February for radiation treatments. The official story was that he was being treated for throat cancer. When Liza heard he was in town, she called him and asked him to go out with her somewhere.

Together they visited some of their favorite clubs. They were photographed at Ellen Greene's opening at Michael's Pub and visited Joan Collins after watching her performance on Broadway in "Private Lives."

On Peter's last night in town, they went back to

Liza's place. Her glamorous penthouse, with its wraparound views of the Manhattan skyline, quartet of Warhol portraits of her, and her shelf of major industry awards, was a far cry from the modest but cozy apartment they'd shared as newlyweds. Had they stayed together, they would have been celebrating their 25th wedding anniversary.

Liza put her arms around Peter and "we just rocked," she later told The Advocate. "He kept saying, 'I'm so sorry. I'm so sorry.' I said, 'You haven't cried about the "throat cancer" at all, have you?' He said no. I finally said, 'Now, I have to tell you two things: One, I love you. Two, you know that I have never said anything about you to anyone, and I'm not going to now.' He said, 'I know.' I said, 'Are we talking about more than throat cancer here?' He said, 'Yes, darling.' I said, 'OK, that's all I want to know.' And that was it. Three days later he died."

Billy's early career as a cabaret entertainer parallels Peter's, but he benefited from the intimate relationship with Liza that Peter did not have. He was photographed frequently with the star and her glamorous friends. He was at Liza's side when she cut her 46th birthday cake at the Desert Inn in Las Vegas in March. A few weeks later, Liza brought him to Hollywood, where she teamed with Shirley MacLaine as a presenter at the Academy Awards. She also brought Billy to London, where she was performing in a tribute to Sammy Davis Jr. There, she was shaken by the news that Ben Vereen, who was also scheduled to perform, had to cancel his appearance. On June 9, her old friend had been critically injured when he was hit by a car while walking on a Malibu road.

The tribute was a rare chance for Liza to work with Lorna, and afterward, the two sisters planned to vacation alone together in Europe. Lorna was about to make a life-changing decision, and it's likely she wanted to talk to Liza about it.

In August, the news broke that Lorna had separated from her husband of 17 years. The children stayed with Jake Hooker while Lorna flew to New York to begin rehearsing for her role as Adelaide in the road company of "Guys and Dolls." She hoped to eventually take over the role when Faith Prince left the Broadway company. While she was in New York, Lorna stayed at Liza's apartment.

"Liza is my best friend and the only person I know I can tell anything to," Lorna said a few months later. "She never judges me. It's really corny, but she's like a part of me."

On Sept. 12, 1992, Liza attended the 9th Annual American Cinema Awards at the Beverly Hilton. Under the direction of David Gest, the American Cinema Awards had been steadily growing in prestige, and the glittering annual gala was beginning to challenge the Oscars and Golden Globes for star power. In 1992, the honorees were Jack Valenti, president of the Motion Picture Association of America, Whoopi Goldberg and Frank Sinatra. With Robert Wagner chairing, Liza of course agreed to be on the committee. She had little to do with the day-to-day business of putting the event together, which is why she barely said more than hello to young Mr. Gest when she arrived for the ceremony.

Romantically, she was still focused on her relationship with Billy.

In January, a clean and sober Liza sounded strange as she spoke to fans while signing autographs at a record store in Philadelphia. She'd had a tooth extracted without painkillers or whiskey, she said. "I'm a good girl now," she insisted.

Liza made a special trip to Houston to catch Lorna's opening in "Guys and Dolls" on January 23. After the show, the sisters and their new beaus, Billy Stritch and Collin Freeman, shared dinner. Liza's relationship with Billy was so serious that they stayed together at his parents' home in Sugarland.

Liza's friend, the socialite Lynn Wyatt, threw a Sunday brunch for the sisters at her River Oaks mansion. The afternoon ended with Billy at the piano and Liza singing, just like one of those Sundays at Sammy's that Liza treasured from her childhood.

In March 1993, Liza celebrated her 47th birthday, an especially significant milestone for her, because that was Judy's age when she died. From now on, when friends tried to get Liza to confront her about her behavior, she would tell them, "I've made it past 47 — I'm doing fine."

At the end of that month, Liza did a song-and-dance number about women and power at the Academy Awards ceremony. The lyrics, by Fred Ebb, included a reference to Hillary Clinton, and a few days later, Liza received a phone call from the first lady herself. "Hello, Liza," she said. "I thought we should meet."

The result was that when Liza and Charles Aznavour appeared together in Washington, D.C., that June, Liza spent the night at the White House as a guest of President and Mrs. Clinton.

In October, Liza dodged death in a rockslide. A

giant boulder came tumbling down toward her as she bicycled along a mountain road in Utah, where she was filming "Parallel Lives," a new movie for cable TV. The boulder missed the star and hit the front of her bike, throwing her smack on her head. Luckily, she was wearing a helmet and escaped with only bruises.

Liza recovered quickly and rejoined the all-improv film, being shot in Salt Lake City. Also in the cast of "Parallel Lives" were old friends Dudley Moore and Robert Wagner. The story centered on the reunion of alumni of a college fraternity and sorority that stirs up old rivalries. Production notes promised that "friendships are renewed, secrets revealed and love declared." The film aired on Showtime Aug. 14, 1994.

That year, Liza was hit by the appearance of another unauthorized biography. "Liza: Born a Star" by Wendy Leigh, revisited her drug problems and failed marriages, most of which was public knowledge.

The freshest material came from Leigh's interviews with one of Liza's former stepmothers and her estranged half sister, Tina Nina. Few people remembered that Liza had another sister, and the star seemed to prefer it that way. Leigh told the New York Native that the only unflattering picture that emerged in her research on Liza was her relationship with Tina Nina. It represented a lifetime of jealousy over Vincente that culminated in Tina Nina's lawsuit over his will.

Yet Leigh came away feeling admiration for Liza. "Yes, she is a sad figure, but she has also fought against tremendous liabilities — from her own addictive personality to her inability to make wise choices. Yet she is making it to those AA meetings. She's still in there fighting."

*Welcome to Hollywood: Liza May Minnelli was born into a
world of brilliance, bisexuality and betrayal.
Pictured above with her mother, Judy Garland*

A Hollywood birthday party for 5-year-old Liza — complete with pony ride (above) and puppet show (above right) arranged by actress mom Judy Garland and director dad Vincente Minnelli

Eight-year-old Liza and her younger sister, Lorna, enjoy a
screening of the Wizard of Oz. Lorna would later
write a scalding biography about the family

An exuberant and happy 12-year-old Liza dancing with her father, Vincente

Eighteen-year-old Liza guest-starred on "The Judy Garland Show" in 1964

The whole gang (from left to right above): Peter Allen, Judy, Mark Herron, Chris Bell and Liza at the airport. Liza and first husband, Peter Allen, sit with matchmaker Judy (left). Despite suspecting Allen to be gay, mom pushed Liza into the marriage

*Peter and Liza on their wedding day –
tender in public but not in private*

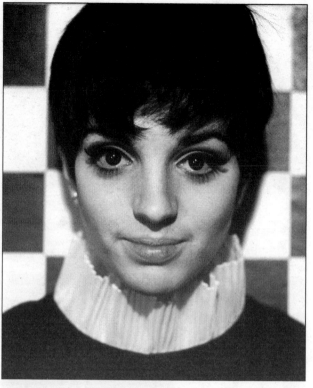

A stylish and thin Liza in the late '60s (above) and with husband Peter Allen in Florida (left)

After some 20 suicide attempts, Judy Garland died of a drug overdose on June 22, 1969. Liza attended the funeral with her godmother, Kay Thompson, and her sister Lorna

Liza with director Bob Fosse. Their work together on Cabaret would earn Liza an Academy Award

Golden girl – Liza proudly displays the Oscar she won for her work in "Cabaret"

Liza with Desi Arnaz Jr., son of Desi Arnaz and Lucille Ball

Liza with Peter Sellers, comic star of the popular Pink Panther movies

"Rex (Kramer) was a super stud," said a bandmate of the young musician who carried on a steamy affair with Liza

Liza gets hitched again – this time to filmmaker Jack Haley Jr.

Partying in L.A. (from left to right) Candice Bergen, Jack Haley Jr., Liza and father Vincente

Partying in N.Y. (from left to right) Halston, Bianca Jagger and Andy Warhol. Liza and Jack share a moment in the background

Three legends in New York, New York –
Martin Scorcese, Liza Minnelli and Robert De Niro

Liza enjoys her
three favorite
hobbies: smoking,
drinking and men
(She is pictured
with designer
Halston)

Liza performs in "The Act" wearing a costume created for her by Halston. She would receive a Tony for best actress in a musical in 1978

Liza in a late
'70s disco daze
at Studio 54
with boyfriend
Mikhail
Baryshnikov

The singer with godmother Kay Thompson and Baryshnikov leaving Studio 54 (right). Sister Lorna, her husband Jake Hooker and Liza enjoy a laugh at the club (below)

Liza and Liz Taylor with Betty Ford at Studio 54

Liza takes a moment with Studio 54 owner
Steve Rubell, who would die of AIDS in 1989

*Liza and sculptor Mark Gero show their moves at Studio 54.
Her marriage to Gero would be her longest – 13 years*

*Vincente, Liza
and Gero pose for
a photographer at
Studio 54 (above)
Liza and Mark
enjoy some
private time (left)*

Always the performer, Liza is once again the center of attention at Studio 54

Liza and Goldie
Hawn perform in
a special for CBS.
The actress with
actor Dudley
Moore in the 1981
movie Arthur
(below)

Vincente and Liza wave for a photo shortly before his death

Michael Jackson accompanies Liza and widow Lee Minnelli at Vincente's memorial service

Liza with ex-hubby Peter Allen in 1987 (above) and with Burt Reynolds (right). She performs with Rat Packers Frank Sinatra and Sammy Davis Jr. (below)

At the White House: (from left to right) composer Marvin Hamlisch, Nancy Reagan, singer Vic Damone, Liza and Bobby Short. Liza enjoys a night out with Billy Stritch in 1996 (above). Liza after hip surgery (right)

*Liza in 1996 – she was frail, tired and worn out –
"An accident waiting to happen"*

*Liza in 1997, after her
second hip surgery*

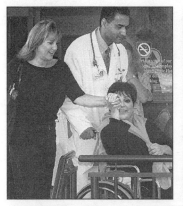

A joyful reunion with sister Lorna (above) after Liza's near-death brush with encephalitis.

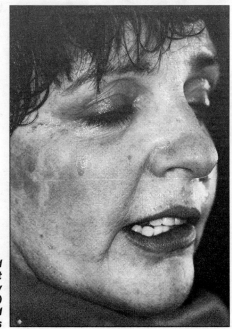

Liza's bloated appearance at the 2001 Tony Awards (right) worried long-time fans

Pushing 200 pounds – unable to perform – Liza consoled herself with food and her cairn terrier until she met David Gest

An exuberant and healthy bride

To counter rampant rumors that David Gest is gay, the bride and groom announced, "We have the most delightful sex life"

At the time Leigh gave the interview, it looked as if Liza was winning her valiant struggle to stay clean and sober. Unbeknownst to anyone, she would soon face a series of health crises and relapses that would nearly kill her.

A twist in her sobriety

"I took coke only on weekends."

Liza's relationship with Billy Stritch and her immediate dreams of parenthood ended at the start of 1994. When she needed a date for the Commitment to Life benefit, an AIDS fund-raiser in Hollywood, she turned to old flame Desi Arnaz Jr. Twenty years earlier they had conducted a very public romance from London to Tokyo, until she had publicly humiliated him by taking up with Peter Sellers. The two arrived arm in arm at the January 27 fund-raiser.

Desi's wife later revealed that Liza had checked with her first, but at the time they attracted plenty of attention from the Hollywood gossip mongers, sharing three romantic dinners in one week and appearing to be very much absorbed with each other during a late-night supper at the hot spot Tatou.

Liza kept busy professionally with more concerts in Chicago, Boston, New York, Cincinnati and Europe. She was also concerned with Kay Thompson's failing health. When her elderly godmother was hospitalized in New York, Liza was a constant loving presence at her bedside when she was in town and called regularly when she wasn't.

In May, Liza was spotted at the MAC makeup shop in Beverly Hills, where she asked the demonstrators to give her the works. Three specialists waited on her hand and foot, and Liza loved the results, but to their shock and dismay, Liza merely thanked them and walked out. Unlike her friends Frank and Sammy, she had never been a generous tipper.

In a typical show of affection for gay publications, Liza sat down for a candid interview by Pulitzer Prize-winning playwright Tony Kushner for Out magazine. "I'm not a drama queen," Liza insisted. "I'm not attracted to pain. I don't go toward it." Keeping to her hectic schedule, Liza was seen everywhere over the next few months. In June, she was part of Broadway's annual Tony Awards. In August, she turned up again, holding hands with Barry Krost, her manager, at the premiere of her TV movie, "Parallel Lives." In October she appeared with George Hamilton at the annual Thalians Ball in Los Angeles. Finally, in December, when Liza was photographed arriving at the Los Angeles airport, leaning on the arm of her friend Veronique Peck (wife of Gregory) and walking with a cane, she announced, "This is the last time you'll see me for a while."

What no one knew at the time was that Liza was in terrible, constant pain. Years of high kicks, combined with a degenerative arthritis condition, had ruined her right hip joint. For 10 years she had suffered in silence. "I was ashamed of it," she later acknowledged. "I don't know why."

On Dec. 17, 1994, Liza had surgery at Century City Hospital to replace her right hip. Her doctor was the same one who had operated on Elizabeth Taylor nine months earlier. Unfortunately, Liza's recovery would prove even rockier than Elizabeth's.

At first, she stunned friends by getting on her feet just three days after surgery and leaving the hospital in time for Christmas. "I feel so much better I can't tell you," she said at a news conference in the hospital lobby. Liza was soon busy planning a tour, a film, an album and a television special. It would all prove to be too much, too soon, however.

Temporarily unable to dance or even to get out to the clubs she loved, Liza was isolated inside the $2 million home in Hollywood Hills that she had purchased from Cheryl Tiegs. She began tossing raucous parties every Saturday night.

Within three months of her hip surgery, Liza was working on a CBS-TV movie, "West Side Waltz," with fellow Oscar winners Kathy Bates and Shirley MacLaine. The movie would air on Nov. 23, 1995. The script was by Ernest Thompson, who had won an Academy Award in 1982 for "On Golden Pond." The role was anything but glamorous. A haggard-looking Liza played a drab violinist who is the only friend of reclusive pianist Shirley MacLaine until MacLaine befriends young, peppy Jennifer Grey. Kathy Bates played a homeless woman.

Meanwhile, the rising young Hollywood producer,

David Gest, was the guest of daytime drama doyenne Ruth Warrick at a state dinner honoring German chancellor Helmut Kohl at the White House in February 1995. Warrick was one of only a few people from the entertainment business to be invited to the dinner. The Washington Post described her as "a fellow traveler on Clinton's 1992 campaign bus, and far and away the grandest dame of the evening in ruby satin trimmed with matching ruby fox." Singer Tony Bennett entertained after dinner in the East Room.

While Gest hobnobbed with Tony Bennett, Henry Kissinger and Secretary of State Madeline Albright at the White House, Liza was sharing a late-night Valentine's Day dinner with Sean Penn at the Bel Age hotel. Liza wore a red mini and they held hands across the table. By the time they finished eating, it was so late that the place was empty and they were allowed to light up for a puff.

In March, Liza called Scott Baio, the handsome former star of "Charles in Charge," whom mutual friends had introduced her to earlier, and invited him to a party at her house. Baio, who rose to fame playing Chachi on "Happy Days," was currently starring with Dick Van Dyke in another TV series, "Diagnosis Murder." He was 16 years her junior, but that didn't discourage Liza.

At Liza's party, Baio met another older woman, Beverly D'Angelo, 40, who had starred with Chevy Chase in the National Lampoon "Vacation" movies. "Scott didn't make any moves on either of them at the party," a source disclosed. "But the next day, he called Liza and asked, 'Would you like to go out to dinner with me?' Liza accepted right away. And they had such a good time, they started a romance. But at the same time, Scott began dating Beverly, who'd recently broken up with a boyfriend."

Liza and Baio kept their romance quiet at first, but they went public in June, when they attended an AIDS fund-raiser dinner at the Beverly Hilton Hotel on the 17th, and were seen again at the Vision Awards two days later.

"They behaved like lovestruck teenagers. They were all over each other," said one insider. "Although there's a 16-year age difference between them, you'd never have guessed."

"I'm nuts about Scott," Liza told a pal. "I haven't felt like this in years. I'm in love and it feels wonderful."

"I know Scott's been out with Liza and I know he dates Beverly," the actor's mom, Rose Baio, admitted. "He's not a kid anymore, so I have to respect his privacy. I don't dare ask for an explanation."

Observers speculated that although Liza would have liked exclusive rights to Scott, she realized the only way she could have him was if she shared him with Beverly. Baio had assured a friend that "unlike so many younger women, Liza doesn't mind if I play the field."

Around this time, Liza got the idea for her first album in years. She was riding in a car in Los Angeles one day when Johnny Mathis singing "Chances Are" came on the radio. "I thought, hey," said Liza, "I experienced my first kiss to that song. We were passing a record store and I stopped and went inside. I asked the clerk for the romance section." The clerk had no idea what she was talking about. She began to think that romance was missing from a lot of people's lives.

Working with Billy Stritch as associate producer, pianist and arranger, Liza started putting together the album that would become "Gently," beginning with a duet with Johnny Mathis on "Chances Are."

Almost a year after her surgery, Liza's dramatic weight loss became evident when she showed up looking haggard at a music industry gala at New York's Plaza Hotel in a lavender gown that Halston had designed for her in 1967.

"She looks so thin," remarked onlookers, many of whom were younger than Liza's dress. "Her face is full of lines," added an acquaintance. "She is not the same Liza we knew before. She is a shadow of her former self."

"Her voice is nowhere near as strong as it used to be," noted another longtime observer. "She talks of her new record as being a 'makeout' album, full of soft songs which are much easier on the vocal cords than her trademark showstopping belters."

But Liza insisted that there was nothing wrong and at 49 she was happy with her looks. "I am feeling fine," she insisted. "Hip replacement is a wonderful operation."

"She is bounding from coast to coast, always on the go," said a pal. "She insists that she likes her new look and is pleased she got the pounds off. But a lot of people think she has taken too much off too quickly."

Liza's spokeswoman, Carol Stone, addressed the concerns. Although Liza had lost weight, it was just by "being able to exercise after being laid up after the hip operation. Right now, Liza is down to her fighting weight. She is fit and she is raring to go. I think she is looking great."

Liza put a halt to her Saturday night house parties as her weight continued to plunge. "Liza just won't eat," said a worried pal. "She sits down and picks at her food. Then she'll get up without eating a thing. Besides that, Liza is pushing herself to get in shape after her hip replacement. She's exercising and doing therapy to get back in top physical condition. She needs to eat more and keep some meat on her bones."

Her friends' concern increased when Liza showed up for a 1996 Academy Awards bash with her hands trembling so badly that she couldn't peel the cellophane off a copy of her "Gently" CD.

By April the once vivacious, robust Liza had become an emaciated shell of her former self. Observers were terrified that she would soon come to the same tragic end as her mother. It was obvious that Liza had fallen off the wagon, and her battle with drugs and alcohol bore a chilling resemblance to her mother's tormented struggles.

One heartbroken family member said, "I'm just waiting for a phone call from some reporter telling me that Liza's dead. I've seen this movie before and I know how it ends. All we can do now for Liza is pray for her. Liza looks just like her mother did in the last months of Judy's life . . . thin, tired, worn out, with that dead look behind the eyes. It's frightening."

Another source noted, "She's very frail, with dark circles under her eyes. It hurts those who love her to see her this way. Liza has worked like a dog in the last year and she's been sick, too. Yet she won't let up."

Her ex-husband, Jack Haley Jr., and her sister Lorna confronted Liza, begging her to get help before she destroyed herself. "Jack pleaded with Liza to come to her senses and take care of herself. He told her, 'Darling, I don't want you to end up like your mom did, but I'm very worried that the same thing is happening to you.' "

Liza furiously denied that anything was wrong with her. After that she stopped speaking to Lorna, blaming her for arranging the intervention. Liza also distanced herself from her kid brother, Joey, who idolized her. Most nights Liza stayed up, calling people all over the world and talking for hours about nothing. She slept all day, not getting up until about three in the afternoon. An insider said that she "mainly eats candy bars and drinks tons of Coke."

Liza seemed increasingly distracted, unable to pull herself together. She was missing plane flights and having to rebook them. At a performance in Miami, she was so verbally abusive to the people who worked with her that nobody wanted to be around.

On the set of the movie "Parallel Lives," sources say Liza was seen scratching herself all over her body. Asked what was wrong, she replied, "I think I have bugs under my skin."

The release of "Gently," Liza's first album in years, had to be delayed because she kept postponing photo sessions for the album's cover. Finally the record company used a four-year-old photo of her just so they could get the album out March 19, a week after Liza turned 50.

A friend added, "I love Liza. We all do. But only one person can help her . . . and that's Liza."

Liza seemed scattered when she sat with a reporter to promote her new CD. She was proud of the liner notes she had written. "Since I had to explain [the

CD's meaning] to myself, I figured, why not to everybody else at the same time?" Liza called it her "makeout" album and joked, "Honey, if you can't get any action out of this, it's just not gonna happen!"

On the eve of an appearance at the Grand in Atlantic City, Liza assured a local paper that she loved the town. "A.C. is homier than Las Vegas. I love the sea, the beach, the boardwalk. I do a lot of work down there. The atmosphere gives me time to rethink some of my projects."

Suddenly, Liza veered off, telling the reporter that she was not thinking about returning to the stage or the screen. Despite rumors that she might be replacing Julie Andrews in "Victor/Victoria," Liza told him there was "no way" she was going to do a Broadway show. "Too hard, man," she said with a laugh.

She wanted to get into the business end, she said, "publishing songs, trying to discover and present talented people, celebrating other people. I've also got a screenplay in the works. Will I ever direct? I don't know. Maybe."

In April 1996, Liza faced more heartbreak when her brother, Joey Luft, was arrested for trying to buy cocaine from an undercover cop. Joey, 42, had worked intermittently as a carpenter, photographer and TV production assistant. Like Liza, he had been in and out of drug rehabilitation centers over the years, but his family believed he was finally clean. They were shattered to learn that he'd relapsed. Sources say he was ordered into rehab and was placed on probation for a year.

Liza may have unwittingly contributed to her brother's problems. Said a family source, "He's always idolized Liza and has been very proud of her career — but her success always accentuated his lack of it. Joey viewed himself as a failure and that caused him to turn to drugs. It's a real shame."

The news could not have come at a worse time for Liza, who was in the middle of her own desperate battle for survival. Photos of a haggard Liza, partying at a Virgin megastore in New York, appeared in May. Friends wished she'd slow down to avoid burning out.

In July, Liza's tangled love life took yet another bizarre turn. Having canceled plans for the 25-year-old Australian actor Simon Crocker to accompany her on a romantic tour of Europe because she realized they were too far apart in age and he was just using her to get acting roles, she invited Cortes Alexander along instead. She'd discovered the handsome 35-year-old when he was singing in a small Greenwich Village club with a group called The Tonics. Soon Liza and Cortes were spotted kissing and holding hands in London. They kept up their embraces when they moved on to Italy, where Liza was scheduled to perform at a charity concert organized by Luciano Pavarotti.

Liza was so wrapped up in Cortes that she was a no-show at a scheduled rehearsal with the famed tenor. Instead, she and Cortes locked themselves away in a $1,000-a-night hotel suite in Bologna and did not emerge until the next morning.

Pavarotti was steaming when Liza finally turned up a day late.

"It was clear to everybody that Pavarotti was barely able to control himself," said his personal photographer, Daniele Venturelli. The tenor's fiancee,

Nicoletta Mantovani, kept him from exploding.

Such trouble seemed miles away as Liza and Cortes enjoyed three days together in Italy. "Liza looked very much in love," Venturelli acknowledged. She and Cortes "held hands, exchanged tender smiles, shared laughs and whispered to each other."

When an Italian reporter asked Liza if she was happy, she answered, "Yes, I'm incredibly happy — because I'm in love."

Privately, she told friends, "I made a silly mistake falling for Simon. He's young enough to be my son and we didn't have anything in common. But I have a great deal in common with Cortes, especially our mutual love of music and singing. He's a sweet, understanding guy and I really love him."

The summer of 1996 soon became a low point for Liza. "She appears like an accident waiting to happen," gossip columnist Mitchell Fink told New York's WCBS-TV. At her July press conference in Munich, Liza appeared clearly disoriented. Published reports said she showed up two hours late, broke down in tears, and sobbed, "My life today is only about my music and the audiences who show up to hear me."

Since Peter Allen's death, lovelorn Liza had bounced from one man to another, including actors Scott Baio and Simon Crocker, and musician Cortes Alexander. It had been 27 years since her mother's death, but now friends feared that Liza's failed love and the strain of touring could send her down the same road.

Not even Lorna could get through to Liza. "Lorna feels Liza's life is out of control and confronted her about it," a friend of both women said. "They had a huge argument and haven't talked since."

Liza's publicist, Allen Eichhorn, insisted that his client was fine and denied the reports that she broke down in Munich. But worried friends urged her to take a two-week vacation before resuming her August concert dates in the United States.

An eyewitness in the south of France that summer was shocked at her appearance. "I couldn't believe how weak and ill she looked," confided the individual, who happened upon Liza while dining out at Le Langoustier, a restaurant near St. Tropez. "She appeared very frail and stressed out. She's lost a great deal of weight and didn't look very healthy. Liza used to look divine. Now she dresses like a bum, and up close, you can see her face makeup is applied in uneven blotches."

In a 1996 interview with The Advocate, Liza said that she had always vowed, "she would never take pills" and then one day she realized that "I was taking a pill for my back, a pill to sleep, a 'terribly innocent, you can't possibly get hooked on them' diet pill because I had gained seven pounds. Finally, I said, 'My God, I am taking pi-I-ills!'" Even so, Liza argued, "I took coke only on weekends, because otherwise you can't sing — it freezes your vocal cords."

In the same interview, Liza addressed the rumors about her and Halston doing drugs. According to her, Andy Warhol got it wrong. She and Baryshnikov were rehearsing for his TV special at Halston's studio, and she was merely teaching him the Charleston when Warhol walked in. Although Halston tried to set him straight, Warhol immediately got on the phone and started spreading the story that they were making love on the table. Later, she acknowledged that she had affairs with Baryshnikov, Martin Scorsese and Peter Sellers.

Liza revealed that with every performance, she was putting money aside for an AIDS hospice she hoped someday to build. It would be one that used alternative medicines. "I already sing in hospices. That's terrific, because then you see the power of music and the power of touch . . . It keeps me attached to all the people I've lost. It reminds me that I have enormous company in my grief."

Liza was soon distressed about another book about her, George Mair's "Under the Rainbow: The Real Liza Minnelli," in which he claimed that Judy had a lesbian affair with Liza's godmother, Kay Thompson. "My mother's name is being dragged through the mud," Liza sobbed bitterly to a friend, "and if my godmother knew what was being written about them, it would kill her. To smear this wonderful old lady's name is sinful. Kay was Mama's best friend and she has been my strength over the years. When my mother died and I was deeply depressed, Kay was there for me. She's been my guiding light."

Liza disputed Mair's claim that Judy tried to upstage her at the Palladium and insisted that her mother had been her biggest supporter. "It's true my mother became a lost soul," Liza said. "But she never abused me — and she never stopped loving me. One of my fondest memories is when Johnny Carson asked her on the 'Tonight Show' who her favorite singer was. My mother answered, 'Liza Minnelli.'"

Liza was talking about her mother more and more these days. After a concert in Westbury in October, Liza stunned her audience by returning for an encore and announcing, "I always promised my mother I'd never do this, but honestly, I don't think she'd mind," and then proceeded to sing an a cappella version of "You Made Me Love You," thrilling the crowd.

At the end of 1996, Julie Andrews called Liza and asked for her help. Andrews and her husband, Blake Edwards, had adapted their film "Victor/Victoria" to the Broadway stage. The musical comedy had opened to mixed reviews but sellout houses.

"Help me out!" Andrews begged. "The doctor told me I can keep going for about three more months, and then I have to take a rest. But it may hurt the show if I leave for a full month. Will you take over for a month?"

"For you to heal up? Yes," Liza responded.

As far as Liza was concerned, it was a matter of being part of the theatrical community. She said, "Anyone in the community would have done the same thing for me if I'd asked."

Just a few months earlier Liza had insisted, "I'm not attracted to pain." Now she was volunteering for what would become one of the most painful episodes in her career.

CHAPTER 8

Hitting bottom

"I hit bottom when my co-star Tony Roberts refused to go on stage with me."

At the start of 1997, Liza received good news, she had been nominated for a Grammy for best traditional pop vocal performance. Also nominated were Rosemary Clooney, Bernadette Peters, Natalie Cole and the ultimate winner, Tony Bennett. In addition, "Gently" became her most successful studio album. Billy Stritch had produced the album, and Matt Casella, her musical director, hoped it would get her the kind of cross-generational appeal Tony Bennett had recently managed. "If she could get hooked into MTV or VH1 and do an Unplugged with them," said Stritch, "I think people would be blown away."

The praise from industry peers came as Liza braced herself for her first Broadway role in 13 years. For Liza, stepping into "Victor/Victoria" was all about friendship. She was excited and optimistic and looked forward to working with Tony Roberts, the Broadway stalwart who played Toddy, and Michael Nouri, best known for "Flashdance," who played the gangster lawyer who falls for Victor.

Billy was against it. To this day he still calls Liza's move to step into "Victor/Victoria" "one of the worst decisions that she ever made — to go into a bad show for no reason."

Liza had her first rehearsal with the dancers in late December, then went off to perform for three nights at the Foxwoods casino in Connecticut. From there, she flew to Las Vegas for a New Year's show at Bally's. Liza planned to take over for Julie Andrews from January 7 to February 11. The preopening interviews that Liza gave to drum up interest in the show only raised more questions about her state of mind. Read today, they are clear warning signs that the fragile star was in trouble.

In one interview, Liza dismissed reports about her health problems. "I'm too busy working to pay any attention to what the tabloids say. You just keep going and pray. All you can do is outlive that stuff. I have done over 60 concerts this year. And I have never missed a show."

Unfortunately, the tabloids would turn out to be right.

The demands of the show were enormous. Julie Andrews herself had already undergone two major surgeries during her run. "I had to learn everything so quickly — songs, script, dances, movements," Liza admitted. "And on top of it all, I had to fit this in between all my other bookings. I don't know any actor who wouldn't be happy to have more rehearsal time, but this time it wasn't possible. I can't complain, though. Everything I've asked to have done in the show was done. Dialogue was changed so my character is American. And they've put in more dancing for me, especially in the 'Le Jazz Hot' number."

One reporter who interviewed Liza in her dressing room at Foxwoods noticed her incessant smoking, the sugar she dumped into her coffee and the ice-cream cone she consumed at one o'clock in the morning. "She sometimes seemed skittish, getting lost halfway through a sentence, breaking into a few practice dance steps unexpectedly, and she often appears quite tremulous," wrote the reporter. "Without her makeup, she's wan and lined and desperately fragile-looking."

In a typical broadcast from Liza Land, she claimed that she had just visited her first drag bar to prepare for her role as a man impersonating a woman. Liza had known men in makeup since the day she was born, and as for drag itself, she had been checking out that lifestyle as far back as the 1970s. As for her appeal to gay audiences, "It is something I am grateful for without completely comprehending."

Liza was upbeat when she talked about "Victor/Victoria." "I feel like a racehorse at the gate, you know? I find it exciting, stepping into Julie's show for a month. Broadway's always been my first love."

But the producers were already denying rumors that she had missed rehearsals. "So, she finally shows up and then she announces, 'Let's all go to my place!'" Said one disgruntled cast member. "Guess what? They do, and not only do Liza and some of her colleagues retreat to her abode, but once there, they all get treated to recordings of — Liza Minnelli!"

There was no denying Liza's magic when she stepped onto the stage. Liza was dazzling as she danced in silver sequins in "Le Jazz Hot," one of the highlights of the show. With her new hip she was kicking as high as chorus members half her age and she easily handled her share of the tap numbers.

After the show, hundreds of fans packed into Laura Belle, waiting to salute Liza, who arrived flanked by her new constant companion, Cortes Alexander and her former flame, Billy Stritch. Right now, though, the most important man in her life was "Victor." When Liza appeared svelte, glamorous and jubilant, Liz Taylor reported there was a surge of energy in the room. Liz and Liza stood on one of the elevated banquettes while Liz held Liza's arm in a gesture of triumph.

When the curtain came down and Liza headed for her dressing room, she was stunned to find that bouquets had been delivered to her backstage. There were 27 more waiting for her at her hotel. Liza had the flowers sent to AIDS wards at St. Vincent and St. Clare hospitals.

At the opening-night party, Liza confided that she learned how to play a man by spending time with her old friends Christopher Walken and Harvey Keitel. Things looked bright, and Liza was talking about coming back with a Broadway show of her own. Around the corner from the Marriott Marquis where "Victor/Victoria" was playing, a revival of "Chicago" was at the Shubert Theater. The show Liza saved in 1976 was still packing them in. Liza still hoped that she and Goldie Hawn might star in the movie version.

"I'm dying to do it, but I don't even dare say it out loud for fear it won't happen," Liza confessed. "It's been a long time since a real movie musical came out . . . It's time they started."

Not everyone was in love with Liza's performance. One powerful studio executive complained, "The poor girl hit every note but the right one."

Liza was still a superstar, as she demonstrated at the Marriott Marquis box office. While she was doing eight shows a week, "Victor/Victoria" consistently brought in $750,000 a week — by far the biggest draw on Broadway. But on January 26, the New York Post's Page Six gossip column broke the story that although Liza's leading man, Tony Roberts, had called in sick for some performances, claiming he had the flu, in fact, Roberts was "really just sick of Minnelli flubbing her lines and losing her focus during the show." Roberts only reluctantly confirmed the report, and insisted that he never intended it to become public knowledge.

"I learned a lot of things on stage from Liza that I had never known before, and they have been very helpful in making me a better actor," said the gallant Roberts. "I've never had a hard word with her, believe me. And I love her!"

When Roberts returned to the show at the end of January, he and Liza kissed and made up on stage.

But the next day, a worn-out and hoarse Liza stood center stage at the Marriott Marquis and told the audience that her doctor had advised her not to perform, because she risked losing her singing voice entirely. Her announcement brought a standing ovation from the crowd and shouts of "We love you, Liza!" Understudy Anne Runolfsson went on in Liza's place.

"She's very ill," said Peter Cromarty, a spokesman for the show. "Liza would have loved to come back, and even up until the last minute was hoping she would, but was advised not to."

Liza missed her final performance of "Victor/Victoria." This was her fifth no-show since she'd developed a throat infection. Liza's manager, Barry Krost insisted that the star would like nothing better than to return to the show when Julie Andrews left for good — but only if Tony Roberts bowed out.

His remarks had infuriated Julie Andrews, who apologized to Liza for his behavior. Despite their public goodwill, Liza and Roberts were obviously still fueding, and the producers of "Victor/Victoria" had been quietly searching for a replacement for Roberts even before he clashed with Liza.

Part of the problem was that after a brief period of sobriety, Liza was drinking again. "I started with beer," sources said she would recall years later while in rehab at Smithers. "But it wasn't enough, so I quickly switched to vodka and gin and I'd find myself the next morning having drunk a whole bottle. I didn't even want to go out with friends because I wanted to keep my drinking a secret from everybody.

"I never drank during a show, but the minute the curtain went down, I'd lock myself in my dressing room and begin drinking and then continue drinking alone at home. I was never drunk on stage, but it seemed like I was, because the alcohol was never quite out of my system. The audience noticed because I was often so hung over that I just couldn't perform very well. Then I hit bottom when my co-star Tony Roberts refused to go on stage with me."

A few months after leaving the show, Liza showed a rare flash of bitterness when she talked about her experience. "I went into "Victor/Victoria" in two days. They don't tell you that in the papers," she complained. "Tony said I was the best person he'd ever worked with on stage, and no newspaper has ever reported that, either. They wanted to make it interesting."

Despite the underlying issues, when Liza said she had health problems, she wasn't just making excuses for her absences from "Victor/Victoria." She soon spent four terrifying days in the hospital with a bleeding vocal cord. The 50-year-old singer feared she would never sing again.

"Liza overtaxed her voice while performing in 'Victor/Victoria,' and she was in a lot of pain," an insider revealed. "She was suffering from severe laryngitis and flu symptoms, complicated by coughing that caused a vocal cord to hemorrhage."

In a very low whisper, Liza told a pal, "I'm spitting up blood and my throat feels like it's on fire. I've got to get to a hospital immediately. My biggest fear is that I'll never be able to sing again."

Liza was rushed to Mount Sinai hospital and seen by Dr. Scott Kessler, an ear, nose and throat specialist. He ordered her not to speak, sing or even hum and to rest her voice completely for several weeks until the vocal cord healed. Only then could doctors determine if there was any long-term damage. Liza now had a nurse with her at all times, and communicated only by writing notes.

Lying in her hospital room, Liza thought, "That's it. Never going to sing, never going to dance — it's all over." She would later call this a period of "sheer despair."

In February 1997, Liza had surgery to remove polyps from her throat. Doctors told her to give up alcohol and cigarettes. Even so, she continued to smoke three packs of cigarettes a day.

Liza had endured the breakups of three marriages and three miscarriages. She had no current love affair and no prospect of one. Friends feared she was on the verge of a total breakdown. She was suffering from exhaustion and memory lapses.

"Every day she has to try to convince herself she's not going to go out the same way her mother did," said a friend. "Whenever she looks in the mirror, she sees Judy looking back at her. She hears her mother's voice talking to her."

On top of everything else, Liza was also worried about ex-husband Jack Haley Jr., with whom she had remained dear friends. At 63, the onetime playboy crown prince of Hollywood was a virtual recluse, suffering from diabetes and facing possible double leg amputation.

"Liza was never the same after her breakup with Jack in 1979," another friend confided. "She measured all men by how they stacked up to Jack. When Liza was really down, she could always call Jack. Over the years he's been there for her when times were rough."

Now Liza went on eating binges for emotional relief. She lived on junk food and couldn't get enough sugar. According to another insider, "Liza loses her train of thought in the middle of a sentence. While she was on Broadway she couldn't stay in harmony with her fellow cast members. Her voice flitted all around the note she was trying to find before landing somewhere near it. She couldn't remember her lines and said whatever came into her head.

"Liza is falling apart in front of our eyes. But her closest friends aren't standing idly by and watching her fall. We're desperately searching for ways to rescue her from her twilight world and bring her back into reality."

Late in April 1997, Liza was convinced she could go on performing. In the middle of rehearsals for her next world tour, she was hit by excruciating pain in her right leg. She stopped suddenly and cried out, "What's happening to me? I can't stand this pain!" An eyewitness watched as Liza fell to the floor and began sobbing. "We helped her up," said the eyewitness, "and she hobbled off the stage in tears."

"The pain in my thigh was unbearable," Liza told a pal. "I couldn't believe that something could hurt so much."

Liza was taken to the Hospital for Special Surgery in New York. Dr. Russell Windsor, an orthopedic surgeon, said that her pain was caused by inflammation and bone fragments, and recommended an immediate operation.

"They told me that if the infection spread to the prosthesis [artificial hip] it would require surgery and could be very dangerous," Liza explained to a friend. "When I was told I needed surgery, I panicked. I'm a dancer as well as a singer — that's 50 percent of my act!"

Only seven weeks after her throat surgery, Liza was back in the operating room. More problems developed when the anesthesia tube reinjured her throat. During the operation, Dr. Windsor cleaned out the bone fragments in Liza's right hip. He ordered complete bed rest in the hospital for a week.

The surgery forced Liza to cancel two sold-out performances in West Palm Beach Fla., the planned kickoff to her world tour.

Bouncing back again would not be easy.

"Usually patients can be given Demerol to kill pain while aggressive physical therapy is used to speed healing," explained Dr. Murah Jassy, a top orthopedic surgeon at Massachusetts General Hospital, who did not treat Liza. "But doctors can't give painkillers to Liza for fear of triggering an addiction. And without painkillers her therapy and recovery are going to be much slower than normal."

Liza was determined. "I can't just go onstage and sing. I have to dance! I love to dance!"

Liza's behavior became increasingly erratic in the following months. On Easter Sunday, she went public with a new love, a hotel doorman half her age, when they attended church services together at St. Patrick's Cathedral. A few days later, they were seen at the opening-night performance of a new musical, "Dream." They turned up yet again at the fashion industry's Michael Awards in May.

Liza had been swept off her feet by 24-year-old King Lewis, who was said to be working miracles in restoring happiness to the problem-plagued star. The two had been escaping Manhattan to spend long weekends at a favorite hideaway.

"I feel like a young, giddy teenage girl again," a beaming Liza told an insider. "It must have something to do with spring and falling in love."

A delighted Lewis declared, "Liza is the most wonderful person in the world. We are very close."

They especially enjoyed taking late-night walks on Central Park South with Liza's cairn terrier, Lilli. Lewis wrapped his arm around Liza's waist and hugged her. Liza looked "ecstatic," confided an eyewitness.

Known to his family as "Thunder," Lewis was a former high school track star and graduate of Ithaca College. "My brother is very athletic," said his sister, Michelle Logins, proudly. "He set new state records in some events."

The muscular 6-foot-2 Lewis met Liza when he took a part-time job as a doorman at the Essex House, where Liza was staying while her apartment was being renovated. "King would see Liza coming into the building, always so exhausted and drained. He would quickly take her by the arm, carry any packages and help her up to her apartment. He was always there for her to lean on, physically and mentally," said one insider. "King knows how to draw people out and then gently advise them on how to resolve their problems. He's always so calm and easygoing. Nothing gets him agitated. It seems like a perfect match."

Besides enjoying the attention of a young, handsome man half her age, Liza was now looking forward to her new tour, a one-woman show that was to kick off in late April.

"She's back. She's ready for her tour, and she has several movie offers," a friend said. "She hasn't been this happy in a long time."

More disturbing were reports about her performance at Atlantic City's Hilton the weekend before.

"She couldn't hit a note to save her life. People were

walking out," one disgruntled witness complained to the New York Post. "She stopped in the middle. It was an embarrassment."

During the show, Liza was sipping what she said was Gatorade and explained that she'd recently had throat surgery to remove polyps. Most of the audience was sympathetic and thankful she made such an effort.

"She got a standing ovation," her spokesman added.

Liza's bloated look and raspy voice startled the audience when she appeared on the Rosie O'Donnell Show on June 20. Liza also had a noticeable limp — the result of the painful hip replacement that had not healed properly. A few days later, Liza met with a producer for an upcoming tribute to Ethel Merman. The meeting was a disaster.

"Liza was so disoriented — barely able to string sentences together — that she was axed from the production," an insider revealed.

On the weekend of June 27-29, Liza managed to keep concert dates in Mexico City. Although her fans were enthusiastic, she appeared tired and lethargic. "After her final concert, Liza and her entourage went to Restaurant New Orleans in Mexico City, where she downed two shots of tequila within minutes of arriving," said one eyewitness. "Then she washed down a pasta dinner with what looked like a gimlet. When Liza went to the bathroom after dinner, she had to lean on friends for support. She couldn't stand up by herself."

After Liza checked out of her suite at the Quinta Real, hotel staff found an empty Jack Daniels whisky bottle in the suite's bathroom. Empty mini-bottles of liquor were in the trashcan — along with a package that once held 38 tablets of Halcion, a sedative. Empty boxes of Valium were also found in the bedroom where she slept. Liza was taking a potentially fatal combination of prescription drugs — Halcion, Valium and painkillers — and mixing these drugs with alcohol.

At the time, Liza denied stories that were being said about her. The 51-year-old singer ignored pleas from pals and her sister Lorna to get help. She was telling friends, "I don't give a fig! It's my life and nobody's going to tell me how to live it."

Liza wouldn't listen to anyone, not even her doctors. "Anyone who drinks while taking Halcion and Valium is definitely risking death. It's a recipe for disaster," declared Dr. William Castelli, director of the Framingham Cardiovascular Institute in Massachusetts, who has not treated Liza. "People can die from an overdose because the combination stops their breathing."

On Sunday night, June 1, 1997, Liza pulled herself together yet again. She donned another vintage Halston gown, flashed a big smile for photographers, and attended the Tony Awards with Michael Nouri by her side. Liza had virtually adopted "The Life," a big, old-fashioned musical comedy starring her friend Sam Harris. She was sorely disappointed that the production didn't win an award.

At the curtain call for "The Life" the following evening, the audience gave the entire cast a thunderous ovation. Harris stepped forward and introduced composer Cy Coleman, who in turn announced that Liza was in the audience and had offered to do something special. Soon Liza was on stage with them, dueting with Sam Harris on his Act I showstopper, "Use What You Got."

Liza was made an honorary member of the cast and received her own official "The Life" baseball cap and oversize T-shirt. She then informed the audience that it would have been Judy's 75th birthday and announced that she was breaking her long-ago promise to her mother. "Cy and Billy [Stritch] told me that I'd know when it was time to break that promise. And I think the time has come!" With Stritch at the piano, Liza proceeded to sing Judy's "You Made Me Love You." Later, Liza generously sang on two tracks for the cast album.

Her own return to Broadway had been disappointing, but Liza had lots of plans. She formed a production company to develop a musical comedy that would trace three generations of a theatrical family based on the Minnellis. She did not intend to perform in it herself.

Liza was also still hoping to revive her film career. Her last mainstream movie was "Arthur 2: On the Rocks" in the 1980s and her last television project had been "West Side Waltz" in 1995. She cryptically told interviewers only that there was a "role in development" that she was excited about.

Matt Capsule, the director of Liza's stage show, was helping the troubled star get her act together, both on and off the stage. Matt was an established musical director and choreographer. As the former casting director for the Mickey Mouse Club, he was credited with discovering Christina Aguilera, Britney Spears and Justin Timberlake. By the end of August, Liza had cut back on alcohol and prescription drugs and begun mending her rocky relationship with her family.

"Liza just loves Matt and Matt loves her too," a source declared. "Liza and Matt have been inseparable since May, when her concert tour began. Liza still liked her doorman, King Lewis and would remain friends with him, but her heart now belonged to Matt. Liza needs to have a strong influence in her life and Matt is the man friends and family feel can keep her off the drugs and booze."

"At a backstage party after a recent concert she drank only water — even though there was all kinds of alcohol around her," an entertainment insider said.

Matt was also trying to help Liza mend her rift with her family. She hadn't seen her stepfather, Sid Luft, or half brother, Joey Luft, in over four years. Matt encouraged Liza to end their feud. She called Sid and invited him to come to her Los Angeles opening and then go out with her and Matt after the show. Sid, Joey and Liza had a warm and touching reunion backstage.

Said the source, "Matt could be the man that Liza needs to keep her happy, healthy and hopeful for the future."

But it was impossible to ignore her weight gain. "Fat's Enough," was the headline over one photo of a puffy-faced Liza that summer. "What's with Liza Minnelli?" asked another. "Is that forced smile masking some inner agony — or is she just happily hefty?"

Even worse, Liza's performances were suffering. Variety panned her July 31 appearance at the Pantages Theater in Hollywood. "Unsettling and at times painful to watch, Liza Minnelli's return to the concert stage in the wake of much-publicized troubles on

Broadway and subsequent throat surgery can be summed up in a phrase: ill-advised." The same reviewer also described Liza's costumes as "an assortment of garish smocks that could pass for off-the-rack from Wal-Mart's maternity department, though credited to Donna Langman, Calvin Klein, Donna Karan and Halston."

At one point, Gary Catona, the vocal coach traveling with Liza, was introduced to a reporter in the Pantages lobby. "How did her voice sound tonight?" Catona asked. When told it was a bit wobbly, Catona said, "Did you tell her that? You should've told her that. Nobody tells her the truth. She's got to hear the truth. I can't raise the dead. I can only raise the half-dead. She's got to take better care of herself."

The Hollywood engagement took an odd turn on the final night. Liza closed the show with an a cappella tribute to her mother, but before she launched into "You Made Me Love You," she looked heavenward and mouthed, "Help me, Ma." Maybe Mama was listening, because Liza hit and held every note of the song, something she rarely managed to do those days.

Liza's dubious diet of Coke and ice cream had sent her weight soaring to nearly 200 pounds. Pain from her hip surgery made walking unbearable. The troubled star holed up in hotel rooms drinking dozens of sodas and eating platefuls of bacon. While friends feared her weight was spiraling out of control, her publicist insisted, "If anything, Liza's lost weight."

"I walked into Liza's suite and it looked like a tornado had hit," said one visitor. "Every 10 minutes, Liza would pop open another Coke Classic — she hates the taste of Diet — and take a swig. The room was littered with at least 35 half-finished and abandoned red cans, some spilling onto the rug."

In the middle of the night, Liza would order a plate of nearly every item on the room service menu. "She'd sample everything," said a source. "Her favorite is stacks of crisp bacon. For dessert she likes to blend chocolate and vanilla ice cream as the perfect remedy for the throat soreness that has tormented her."

Back home in New York, Liza continued to pig out. A local grocer regularly delivered the following order to Liza's apartment: Six pints of Haagen-Dazs ice cream (cherry vanilla, chocolate, macadamia brittle, cookies 'n' cream, vanilla, vanilla fudge); 1 quart of Breyer's ice cream (vanilla with Hershey milk chocolate and almonds); 2 pints of Ben & Jerry's ice cream (Chubby Hubby); 2 cases of Coke Classic (12 oz. cans); four 6-packs Coke Classic (8 oz. bottles); 2 liters of Cherry Coke; 7 pounds of bacon; 1 Sarah Lee French Cheesecake; 1 Sarah Lee Fudge Golden Layer Cake; 1 Sarah Lee Double Chocolate Layer Cake; 2 packages of Oreo Double-Stuff cookies; 2 packages of Keebler Chips-Deluxe cookies and 2 packages of Chips Ahoy chocolate chip cookies.

Pals worried that she lacked the emotional support to stop before she ate herself to death. "Liza is acting like her mother, Judy, just before her fatal overdose. She's fragile, vulnerable and very needy," said a friend. "My deepest fear is she may come to the same tragic end."

In spite of the stories, early in October 1997, Liza assured her old friend Maxine Mesinger that she was making great progress in her recovery from throat surgery. "Nobody told me how long I'd have to stay away from singing," said Liza. "So I went back to work when I shouldn't have." But the good news, she assured Mesinger, was that she was much better. She had been in Paris to consult a famous throat doctor, recommended by her friend Charles Aznavour. She was back in her New York apartment with Kay Thompson.

Days later, Liza canceled her third concert series in two months. Sources close to Liza insisted she was still going forward with her planned one-woman Broadway show.

Liza's problems were such an open secret in the business that they became the stuff of a "Saturday Night Live" sketch that portrayed her as a lush who constantly forgot her lines. "It was a low blow," protested Billy Stritch.

By July 1997, it had been 2-1/2 years since Lorna and Liza had spoken. Liza declined to attend a family get-together in Grand Rapids, Minn., to mark what would have been Judy's 75th birthday. Lorna was there with her father, Sid, who was battling colon cancer; her kid brother Joey Luft; and her children, Vanessa and Jesse.

"They were hoping right up to the last moment that Liza would relent and come to this special occasion, but it wasn't to be," said a family friend.

Lorna, now married to Colin Friedman, was still singing. Troubled by the stories about his former stepdaughter, Sid tried to reconcile with Liza and begged her to make peace with Lorna. The sisters had not spoken since Lorna urged Liza to enter rehab. Sid was determined to end the feud before he died.

"It's breaking my heart that there's a rift in this family," Sid confided. "They need each other. Having battled cancer for the past year has made me think about my life and the life of my children. God forbid, if something does happen to me, I don't want to know Liza and Lorna aren't speaking."

Sid had a breakthrough when he and Joey went to see Liza perform in Los Angeles. "Lorna refused to go to the theater," said a close friend of Sid's. "But after the show, Sid brought up the feud and Liza listened. She was open to a reconciliation, but she wouldn't make the first move."

"Pop, I love you and I know how much this means to you," Liza told Sid. "I promise you that I will think about it."

Lorna did not hold out much hope for a reunion. "We have become estranged," was about all she wanted to say, but she added, "We all make our own lives. She decided to make other choices. And that is fine. Maybe someday it will change. She does remember the kids."

In November, pale and overweight, Liza sat for an interview on the nationally syndicated "Gayle King Show." Her purpose in appearing on the show was to dispel rumors that she was in poor health. Unfortunately, the appearance raised more questions than it answered.

Liza and her cairn terrier, Lilli, a dead ringer for Toto, had become inseparable. Liza told Gayle King that Lilli was a reincarnation of Toto and had been sent to her by her late mother. Liza claimed that she and Lilli watched her mother's movies over and over. And if she was out of town for more than a day, she talked to Lilli by phone, singing songs from the "Wizard of Oz" to her. Holding the dog during the interview, Liza told Gayle, "I think I got this dog as a defense mechanism. I got tired of saying, 'No, it's Liza not Lisa.' I can just say 'It's Lilli — not Toto.'"

Friends believed that Lilli was getting all the love Liza would have lavished on a child. She named the dog for the daughter she never had.

According to Dr. Carole Lieberman, a leading Beverly Hills psychiatrist who has not treated the star, Liza's dog had become a link to her mother. "The lonelier a person is, the more they will focus on a pet," Lieberman said. "Also, the business of it reminding her of Toto and her mother is understandable in a way. Liza's belief that Lilli is a reincarnation of Toto is her way of making a connection to her mother."

In December, Liza fell while walking with Lilli and Billy Stritch down a street in Manhattan. She hurt her knee and reinjured the hip she had replaced several years before. After undergoing arthroscopic surgery, Liza was photographed on red crutches when she showed up at the 25th anniversary screening of "Cabaret" in New York. She willingly posed for pictures, but she lost her nerve about going onstage to say a few words and quietly slipped out amid questions about whether the one-time brightest star of Broadway would ever return to the Great White Way.

CHAPTER 9

In the shadows

"What else can go wrong?"

Liza was shaken when her sister, Lorna Luft, finally published her long-awaited family memoir, "Me and My Shadows," in April 1998. At age 30, after a binge left her clinging to a toilet bowl for four days, Lorna quit drugs cold turkey. Lorna was as frank about herself as she was about Liza. After watching Liza destroy herself with booze and coke, Lorna now took a tough-love approach, refusing to see her until she cleaned up permanently.

Lorna did not spare Judy, either. She drew a much more harrowing picture of life with Mama than the one Liza clung to, detailing the night in 1968 when Judy tried to kill their kid brother, Joey, with a butcher knife. Lorna also claimed that she alone took care of Judy in her tragic last days and that Liza, who was working on Broadway, had turned her back on them. She now saw her sister going down the same destructive path that killed their mother, and she refused to be Liza's keeper, too.

Liza tried to remain blase about Lorna's new book, but she was very upset about it. She told a friend, "There's no man in my life. I don't have the kids I always wanted. My own sister hates me. Now the only thing I have left, my talent, is being threatened by health problems that keep me off the stage. I can take the pain but I can't stand the thought of losing my career."

"I feel like everything's ganging up on me again," Liza moaned to another friend. "I have a bump on my right knee and my hip is killing me. I've gained 25 pounds. I'm dying for a cigarette and I'm no spring chicken. What else can go wrong?"

After a year of poor reviews, canceled concerts and illness, Liza opted out of her scheduled appearance at the Academy Awards because of horrible hip and knee pain. She tried to improve her health by giving up smoking, but she replaced cigarettes with more junk food.

When Liza returned to the stage to give three shows at Foxwoods Resort Casino in Connecticut, one writer described her opening night as "a humble and sometimes tortured performance."

She also headlined an event at Tsongas Arena in Lowell, Mass., on February 21. "Vocal and physical limitations affected her overall performance," wrote Boston Herald critic Dean Johnson. The Boston Globe announced, "More painfully noticeable than Minnelli's singing was how out of breath she was after only a few songs."

Liza was forced to cancel several performances she had scheduled for March at the Hummingbird Centre in Toronto and at Bally's in Las Vegas. That set off talk in show business circles that the curtain was about to finally fall on her spectacular career.

In mid-March 1998, Liza was quietly admitted to Columbia-Presbyterian Medical Center in New York. Her spokeswoman, Susan DuBow, told a reporter: "Liza's had a flare-up with her hip and knee. Her tour is not continuing and she's not rebooking any canceled dates at this time."

"We're all scared to death Liza is getting in trouble again," one pal confided amid published reports that she might have returned to rehab. "When she's depressed and in pain, she turns to alcohol and drugs. Every time life gets tough for Liza she slips back into her old habits. Everyone's worried she's secretly sneaking painkillers to ease the strain of everything going on in her life."

Liza was placed in the VIP section of the hospital's McKeen Pavilion, suffering from severe synovitis of the right knee and greater trochanteric bursitis in her right hip. Synovitis of the knee is a swelling of the joint and can be caused by a variety of problems, including overuse, torn cartilage, wrenching or dislocation of the joint, or various forms of arthritis. Trochanteric bursitis is inflammation and pain in the hip joint, and can be caused by the same problems. The ordinary treatment for these conditions is rest and anti-inflammatory drugs. Fluid may be drained and cortisone injected into the joint. If that doesn't work, surgery may be called for.

Those close to Liza advised her to take a long rest,

but Liza insisted, "I don't have a life if I'm not in front of an audience. I need to perform!"

It was almost more than she could bear.

In May, Liza's weight gain shocked photographers when she was trotted out May 5, 1998, for the media while attending a new Broadway revival of "Cabaret."

"Liza quickly put on a jacket to cover up her body from photographers, but she couldn't hide her face. I have never seen her heavier, or her face so swollen," one longtime observer noted.

"She still has pain in her hip and knee, which, requires medication several times a day and causes bloating," a friend explained. "She has erratic sleeping habits and just can't sleep until she passes out, usually at dawn. She stays up watching infomercials. She'll stay in her bedroom and order pizza with four to five toppings on it, and double cheese. She'll lie in bed and eat one whole large pizza for dinner and then want another one around 1 a.m. She washes all that down with Coca-Cola and tops it off with Twinkies."

Sometimes Liza talked about her mother in a way that deeply troubled her friends. She told one friend, "I still have Mama with me. She never leaves my side and she never stops telling me that I'm doing OK and that I'm her little girl. Mama loves the fact that I have my dog, Lilli, who looks just like Toto. In fact, Mama told me to call her Lilli Toto. I'm not a wacko. Mama's there for me in spirit and that gives me a lot of strength because I don't have a lot of family."

According to the friend, Liza detailed the little things she still did with her mother and what Judy was wearing in their recent encounters. Still furious about Lorna's book, Liza sometimes rambled that she was thinking about writing her own book and telling the "real truth," warning, "Maybe Lorna won't come out looking so pure."

There was still hope among her loyal fans that Liza could turn things around. In late May, spokeswoman Dubow stated that Liza had actually lost some weight. "I don't know how much she's lost. The weight loss has occurred recently. She's not on any medication that causes any sort of puffiness . . . She's on the road working. She hasn't stopped. Liza has been working quite a bit . . . As far as Lorna Luft's book is concerned, Liza has already been quoted in the papers as saying, 'I love my sister and wish her the best.' "

Liza was said to be trying to get into shape, pushing herself with a backbreaking string of concerts that could leave her exhausted. "Liza's always talking about taking better care of herself, but she doesn't do it," said an insider who noticed the pattern of empty promises. "She'll talk about getting a personal trainer, then never mention it again. She'll take vitamins for a few days, then forget about them."

Between May and August, Liza was planning on coast-to-coast concerts from Reno, Nev., to Tanglewood, Mass., with a grueling overseas trek in June to perform five shows in eight days in the U.K.

"Unlike most people, who can't wait for vacation, Liza falls apart when she's not working because she just doesn't know what to do with herself," said a friend. "Worst of all, it seems she's constantly eating — she eats cakes and ice cream between meals, then goes out to dinner and always cleans her plate. Having put drink and drugs behind her, food is the only thing Liza has left that gives her the energy to keep going.

The trouble is, she doesn't see that overeating, especially junk food, can be as harmful as other vices."

While Liza struggled with health and career problems, David Gest moved into a lavish new home. He had purchased a two-bedroom, 3,700-square-foot apartment on the 29th floor of the Millennium Towers in New York for $1.9 million and was soon elected to the board of directors. One of his first moves was to evict a neighbor's new puppy. Gest claimed the yellow Labrador was illegal because his owner had not registered the dog with the condo board. Soon, all dogs would be required to wear muzzles while entering and exiting Millennium Towers. One resident complained, "He's a germaphobe who walks around the building in a bathrobe and hospital slippers."

Meanwhile, Lorna was scheduled to sing "San Francisco" and "The Man That Got Away" at a Garland tribute at Carnegie Hall on June 16 and 17. Organizers were still holding out hope that Liza would join the stars, who included Bebe Neuwirth, Robert Morse, Alan King and Elaine Stritch.

Liza's godmother, Kay Thompson, passed away July 2, 1998. Thompson had been more or less a recluse over the last decade while living at Liza's. "Liza's mother, Judy Garland, benefited greatly from Thompson's guidance," wrote one columnist. "Many of Judy's dramatic gestures and a lot of her latter-day vocal style were borrowed from Kay . . . Thompson was famously witty . . . No one who ever saw her nightclub pyrotechnics where she sang and danced with the four Williams Brothers could ever forget Kay."

Since Judy's death, her godmother had been the one

continuous mother figure in Liza's life, but Kay's health had been failing for years. Liza was in Mexico with Tina Nina when the end came. Still reeling from the death of Frank Sinatra, Liza now had to cope with another devastating loss.

"I just can't lose one more person," she sobbed. "Frank was a real blow. Now Kay's gone. Since mama died, I've always had her to help me."

Liza had never forgotten that when her mother died, Kay had swooped in and taken charge, guiding a shell-shocked Liza through a dignified funeral. On Friday, July 10, Liza returned the favor by holding a private memorial for a handful of friends at the Plaza to "sip, sup and remember" her godmother with Kay's favorite songs and stories.

"Kay was so helpful," Liza recalled. "I loved her. I called her every day. When my sister Lorna went against me, Kay said, 'Honey, relax. She'll go through with her agenda no matter what . . . so just relax and hang on to your hair.' It's going to be so hard without her. She left so many little things for me. All wrapped in the red ribbons she loved."

In August 1998, Liza was said to be suffering a flare-up of her arthritis, and doctors ordered her to take a month off from touring. Then Julie Andrews, her own singing voice silenced, asked her to perform in September in her PBS "Great Performances" concert at Carnegie Hall, despite her disastrous experience in "Victor/Victoria." Liza agreed. She was not one to hold a grudge

The concert, "My Favorite Broadway: The Leading Ladies" was a love fest, although the first three divas originally announced, Betty Buckley, Chita Rivera and Anne Reinking, had all dropped out by the time the show was taped on September 28. That made Liza's generous gesture even more important to the show.

Introduced by Rosie O'Donnell, Liza went back to her roots with "Sing Happy" from "Flora, the Red Menace," before launching into "Some People." Theater critic Clive Barnes thought her performance evoked memories of the great Ethel Merman, who had introduced the song in "Gypsy," and he hoped he'd see Liza in her role some day.

The other leading ladies in the show included Jennifer Holiday, Elaine Stritch, Dorothy Louden and Nell Carter. Ironically, newcomers Karen Ziemba and Bebe Neuwirth did a dazzling duet from "Chicago," the show that Liza had waited for years to bring to the screen.

In September, contrary to reports that she was an ailing recluse, Liza was photographed out on the town with Billy Stritch. Bill was with her again when she cheered on Sandra Bernhard at the premiere of her one-woman show, "I'm Still Here, Damn It." By November, Liza was playfully posing in Santa's lap before the opening of Radio City Music Hall's Christmas spectacular. In December, she was at Billy's opening at Joe's Pub, the new cabaret space at the Public Theater downtown. Word was that they would be working together on a new album to follow the success of "Gently."

In her 1996 interview with The Advocate, Liza blamed her problems on menopause. "It gives you enormous mood swings, which nobody told me about. You start out loving somebody at the beginning of a sentence, and by the end you're going, 'You son-of-a-bitch Communist bastard!' You really don't know what's happening."

Liza got another jolt when she learned that Alan Pakula, the man who had directed her in "The Sterile Cuckoo," had been killed in a freak accident on the Long Island Expressway. Pakula, 70, died when a seven-foot steel pipe smashed through the windshield of his 1995 Volvo station wagon and speared him through the head. Pakula had kept an office in Manhattan and was driving to his home on Long Island.

In 1969, the first-time director had believed in Liza enough to cast the youngster in her first important film role. His confidence paid off and she received an Academy Award nomination. It remained her favorite role.

As the holidays approached that year, something was missing for Liza — a family.

"When it comes time for a big holiday and the 'family' is supposed to get together, Liza never gets invited because she has been at war with everyone," explained a friend. Liza had been close to Lorna's two children, once saying to her, "Since I don't have any children, your children are my children," but by now it was four years that the two half sisters had not seen or talked to each other.

Then, just as things had appeared darkest, Liza found new resolve. With the end of another hard year at hand, it looked as if she had conquered her demons and was ready to start a brand-new life. The driving force behind her dramatic turnaround was the hope of adopting a baby.

"A year and a half ago, she was clouded by booze and drugs," said an insider. "Friends feared the worst then, prayed that somehow she'd pull herself out of this downward spiral. But Liza managed to turn herself around. She's got a whole new lease on life. And the main reason is she now has a vision of being a mom."

Liza had been attending AA meetings in New York for months. "Today's Liza is a clean and sober health fanatic," said the friend.

"The only thing missing in my life is being a mother. I've had it all. And now I want a baby to share it with," Liza told a friend. Three miscarriages had left her depressed and numb, because the one thing she wanted more than anything was a baby. "I'm at an age where I know having my own child is out of the question," Liza went on. "But I still can adopt. There's still time."

Liza reached out to friends Rosie O'Donnell and Mia Farrow, wanting to find the happiness she had seen in these two adoptive moms. For years, Mia had been whispering in her ear that adopting a baby would change her life.

Billy Stritch had already agreed to be the adoptive dad, and the two were said to be anxiously awaiting the arrival of the stork.

"I know I'd make a great mother," Liza gushed. "This has given me so much hope."

CHAPTER 10

Liza battles back

"Sometimes God says, 'Slow down –
you've got something important to do.'"

Early in the new year, a radiant Liza Minnelli looked "like a million bucks" after a two-week stint detoxing at a San Diego health spa. The actress had thrown herself into nutritional classes and self-esteem seminars and was following a strict diet of wheat grass juice and raw fruits and vegetables.

Only a few insiders knew that Liza had undergone the very same operation on her vocal cords that had already silenced Julie Andrews. Liza feared that she, too, might never sing again. Ironically, Liza and Billy Stritch blamed "Victor/Victoria" for her vocal problems — both she and Julie Andrews had been diagnosed with the polyps while singing in the musical. They maintained that switching between the male and female voices was very destructive for singers.

Liza told no one at the time, but for two years after

her operation she worked constantly to restore her voice, taking a singing lesson every day. As her 53rd birthday approached, in 1999, Liza began to feel her old self coming back.

One thing that was not coming back, however, was Liza's friendship with Lorna. The feud between the two sisters hit a new low that March. Still angry about Lorna's book, Liza informed the organizers of a London tribute marking the 30th anniversary of their mother's death that she would not perform at the June 27 gala if Lorna was on the bill.

Still, Liza refused to call it a feud. "We're sisters and we're going through something," was all she would say. As for the tribute, "I've never gotten involved in those things. I sometimes resent that they use her for stuff. I don't want to exploit her. I've never exploited either of my parents."

In April, Liza reached out to her ailing friend Dudley Moore. Having battled back from health and substance abuse problems, she was trying to get him to do the same. She had been talking with the depressed actor daily since Barbra Streisand fired him from "The Mirror Has Two Faces" in 1996 because he could not remember his lines. Liza vowed she would take him on tour with her once he was back on his feet.

That month, a group of New York's cabaret and nightclub performers and their supporters gathered to honor Liza at Town Hall. Those at the Annual Manhattan Association of Cabarets Awards ceremony could not hide their shock at her weight gain, but Liza kept a sense of humor. Picking up her award, she cracked, "This is a great honor for me — particularly this year, when there's so much more of me to appreciate."

Liza added, "Just watching you get up there and do it makes me want to get up there and do it. I love you. You have my admiration. You inspire me more than I can possibly tell."

Then she launched into "Stormy Weather" and brought down the house. Poor Betty Buckley had the hard luck to follow her, giving a polished performance of "Serenity" to an audience that Liza had wrung out and left to dry.

The ever loyal gossip columnist Liz Smith announced that Liza's performance at the MAC awards that afternoon was only "the first layer of the great comeback cake this grand star has been cooking for herself." The icing would come in May, when Liza was scheduled to begin rehearsing "Minnelli on Minnelli," the new Broadway show she was putting together with her longtime musical mentors John Kander, Fred Ebb and Marvin Hamlisch.

At one point at the MAC Awards party, Liza was stopped by a Judy Garland impersonator, Tommy Femin, who joked, "Everything would be fine as long as Lorna doesn't write another book. Who knew she could write? Who knew she could read?"

Liza reportedly laughed, proving that she still had her sense of humor, even about such a sensitive subject.

Until that dazzling performance at the MAC Awards, even longtime friends such as Fred Ebb had doubted that Liza would make it back. "At one point it was very dicey whether she would perform again," he later admitted. "She wanted very much to do ["Minnelli on

Minnelli"] and knew that I was reluctant to do it because I was unsure whether she could perform . . . My love for her never wavered, but professionally I wondered whether I should be doing it."

When Liza had approached Ebb about her idea for a tribute to her father, he told her that he would do it if only she assured him she would get herself into shape. "I told her if I couldn't sit in a room and listen and be proud of her, I'm out. I said, ' I don't want to see you fail.' "

But with her performance of "Stormy Weather" at the MAC Awards, Liza stood him on his ear. "This was a tough crowd," Ebb recalled. "I was crying, everybody was crying. I went backstage, and she said, 'Well, do I get the job?' "

Liza was back, yet again!

By spring, Liza had passed a physical examination that included a drug test and was deep in preparations for her big millennium show. The plan was for Liza to ring in 2000 by performing in Europe and America. The diva would sing in Paris, then fly to New York aboard the Concorde, arriving in time for midnight with her second show of the evening. Once she arrived in New York, a helicopter would whisk her to a landing pad near Carnegie Hall, where she would be rushed onstage.

This idea was discarded as Liza threw herself into plans to return to Broadway.

"Liza has shocked everyone," said a source close to the star. "She had lost her voice and canceled show after show. She started hiding out in her apartment. She looked like a stuffed sausage whenever she squeezed into an old dress. She didn't listen to the pleading from friends. But one day something snapped and she realized she had hit rock bottom. She couldn't go any lower unless it was six feet under."

Liza hired a top vocal coach, Joan Kobin, who became a surrogate mother. Diligent and patient Joan encouraged the star to find the energy to help herself. Feeling great and sounding superb, a jubilant Liza told a friend, "For the first time, I can truly say, I'm in love with life. I want to live."

Unfortunately, Liza would hit a pothole on the road to happiness. Trouble began in early June, when she returned to Hollywood for a series of parties honoring her as a model of sobriety in show business. The trip was a disaster.

Liza and her constant companion, Lilli the cairn terrier, were booked into the $2,500-a-night luxury suite at the elegant Peninsula Hotel. Burt Reynolds, her old friend and co-star had organized an A-list of entertainment industry stars to honor Liza on Sunday night, June 6. The crowd that gathered at Chasen's included Raquel Welch, Joan Collins and Jon Voight. Liza herself had invited her former stepfather, Sid Luft, and kid brother, Joey Luft, with whom she had recently reconciled.

But the evening had hardly begun when a steamed Reynolds, speaking with clenched teeth, announced that "Liza's people" had called at the very last minute to inform him that she had "a bad case of food poisoning." The Lufts were as shocked as Reynolds, who left early. By 9 p.m., the room was empty. People wondered whether Liza would make it to the highly-touted dinner at the Beverly Hilton ballroom the following night.

To everyone's surprise, Liza did make it to the black-tie event sponsored by Recording Artists, Actors and Athletes Against Drunk Driving, chaired by David Niven Jr. She even got up to belt a few numbers, accompanied by Michael Feinstein and Billy Stritch, but at least one ear-witness complained, "her voice sounded like it belonged to somebody else."

Liza concluded her performance by telling the star-studded crowd, "Here's to life and health and staying sober."

A few hours later, she was spotted partying up a storm at the Peninsula. "I saw Liza twice in the hotel bar, and she was stumbling drunk both times," said an eyewitness. "She looked bloated and bleary-eyed. She was drinking vodka. She slumped into a friend of mine to avoid falling on her face."

The partying continued up in Liza's hotel room. All the miniature liquor bottles had to be replaced two or three times, and she ordered Cristal champagne, 20 ounces of Beluga caviar and a bottle of vodka through room service.

Liza left the suite in a shambles, burning a hole through a duvet cover because she was smoking in bed and allowing Lilli to turn a bed and sofa into her personal powder room.

As stories like this reached Lorna, she made one more try at ending their feud. She knew that Liza blamed her and Sid for exploiting Judy Garland's name. But Lorna felt that she was merely telling her personal story. "I was not a nonentity," she explained. "I had a story to tell. I mean Frank Sinatra was my godfather and I hung around with very famous people. I lived in a world not many people get to see, but was normal to me. I feel I have a license to show people what it was like."

Lorna invited Liza to join her on stage for the benefit at the London Palladium on Sunday, June 27, marking the 40th anniversary of Judy's debut there.

"Lorna pulled out all stops," said one of the few friends still close to both sisters. "She wanted Liza to be on stage with her. She believed that it could break the ice between them and make them a family again."

But at 1 p.m. on Monday afternoon, June 21, Liza's housekeeper found her unconscious and frothing at the mouth on the floor of her East Side apartment. A private car was called and Liza was rushed to the nearest hospital, St. Luke's Roosevelt, 10 blocks away, where she was admitted to a private room on the 14th floor. In spite of eyewitness stories, Liza and her publicist vigorously denied that she was ill. But Liza would spend the 30th anniversary of her mother's death writhing in a detox ward as doctors fought to save her after a near-fatal alcohol overdose.

While not exactly denying the hospitalization, Liza said in a statement, "I want the people who care about me to know I'm taking care of myself. I'm looking forward to performing again and giving back to my fans and friends the love they have shown me by being healthy. I feel there is no shame in taking positive action."

After her release from the hospital, Liza decided that to stay sober, she had to get professional help. She entered the Smithers Alcoholism Treatment Center, an outpatient clinic at St. Luke's Roosevelt. "It's not an easy thing for me," she told a friend. "But I'm sure I'm going to make it this time. I just have to, for my own good."

Soon, Liza was deep in therapy at Smithers. "She hasn't missed a day in four weeks," a source confided. As part of the program, Liza followed the 12 steps of Alcoholics Anonymous. Insiders said that Liza had also "found God." She was said to be carrying a Catholic rosary and embraced the AA motto, "Let Go and Let God." She was also just one of the gang at the AA meetings, often joining fellow members for smoking breaks on the sidewalk outside the clinic's entrance.

On weekdays, she was at Smithers from 8:30 a.m. until noon. Afternoons were free for rehearsal. On weekends, Liza saw a private counselor just to make sure she didn't fall off the wagon. Said a source, "Liza's goal is to be A-OK for the Broadway opening of 'Minnelli on Minnelli.' "

During treatment, Liza finally acknowledged that for years she had been tormented by guilt. She blamed herself for Judy's death. Liza had bottled up her guilt and anger for years, and now in therapy it was all coming out. Suppressing those feelings for so many years was what made her drink, she said.

Liza made a startling confession to her fellow alcoholics at Smithers: "I could've saved my mom from killing herself," she said, "Sometimes I wouldn't even take my mother's phone calls because I knew she was loaded. It killed me to ignore her, and it never stops haunting me that if I had tried harder, I could've saved her. I feel so horribly guilty because we were so close and I was my mother's caretaker."

For the first time, Liza even admitted that she had some doubts that her mother's fatal overdose was accidental.

During one group therapy session, a patient

revealed that Liza broke down in tears and began speaking to Judy. "I need to confront you," she said. "Stop pretending that you don't need help and can take care of yourself, because that's a lie! You needed help and you kept pushing it away. It was just killing me to watch you overdo it and act like you were fine. You'd hide drugs all over the place. I knew you loved me, but if you really loved me as much as you said you did, why couldn't you stop for me? Why couldn't I stop you? I feel horrible about that."

By October, Liza was at least 30 pounds lighter, her eyes were bright, and she had 90 days of sobriety under her belt — the longest she had gone without a drink in decades. She was ready to hit the stage in "Minnelli on Minnelli" scheduled to open in New York December 1.

She told the group, "I'm happier now than I can ever remember."

A fellow patient said, "Liza looks good and obviously feels great. She's very down to earth. She doesn't act like a big star who expects to be treated differently than the rest of us. She's friendly and shows concern for other people's problems. Everyone in the group is rooting for her and is really proud of the progress she's made."

At the same time, Liza was anxious to continue her "normal" life. In September she was photographed out and about and was seen chatting with comedian Alan King at the U.S. Open. King had appeared with her mother at the Palace Theater.

Liza started her day dressed in sweats and Gucci sunglasses for a power walk in Manhattan's Central Park. When she returned to her Upper East Side apartment, her housekeeper prepared her an egg-white omelet, a slice of toast, orange juice and coffee. Next, a trainer put her through her paces, with stomach crunches and weight training.

Three times a day, she practiced meditation to help her relax, and she had also cut back on her drinking. Her hard work was paying off. She showed off her new figure at a luncheon at the 21 Club. The posh eatery tested Liza's willpower, but she passed. "She ordered a salad," said one source. "The rest of her party ordered steaks. But Liza didn't seem to mind." Friends prayed that Liza's new healthy lifestyle would stick this time.

"Unlike her poor mama, Liza's always had luck on her side," said one pal. "She always seems to bounce back."

In October, having lost 40 pounds through a high protein diet and killer training program, Liza held a press conference to talk about "Minnelli on Minnelli," the musical based on her father's most memorable films that was scheduled to open on Broadway December 8. While she'd been immobilized by her hip and knee surgeries, she had watched her father's films. Getting reacquainted with her father's work "helped me so much. Sometimes God says, 'Slow down, you've got something important to do.' I feel like this was meant to be."

She had never sung half the songs from her father's films in her performances. Nothing from "Meet Me in St. Louis," "Kismet," "Cabin in the Sky," "Ziegfeld Follies' or "An American in Paris." She explained, "I've never exploited either of my parents. What I'm doing in 'Minnelli on Minnelli' is a celebration."

Late 1999 found Liza coming to grips with her

alcoholism. She talked about her drinking problem on "20/20," saying she had found peace by reciting AA's famed prayer, which begins, "Grant me the serenity to accept the things I cannot change . . ." She added her own line: "Let me just do what I was put here to do."

Dr. Lois Mueller, a psychologist in Tampa, Fla., explained that Liza's public admission could be a gigantic step to conquering her demons. "Bravo for Liza," said the therapist. "Most alcoholics — like her mother, Judy Garland — live in denial. They won't admit to themselves that they have an addiction problem so they keep hiding their pain in liquor and drugs. Liza's honesty is her salvation."

Asked what she was doing to maintain her sobriety, Liza responded, "I do everything. Go to meetings, study the Dalai Lama, discipline my eating and drinking. I'm up at 7 a.m. to rehearse all day. I'm taking singing, dancing and remembering Martha Graham's mantra: Can't do at 30 what you did at 20, can't do at 40 what you did at 30. If I go out, it's a quick night. By 8 o'clock, I'm gone."

On December 1, Liza gave her first preview performance of "Minnelli on Minnelli." It was a comeback to Broadway and to the Palace Theater, where her mother had once staged a famous comeback. Written and directed by Fred Ebb, the show had Liza, in a series of black and silver Bob Mackie pant suits, reminiscing a bit, showing pictures from the family album, and singing numbers made famous by her mother that she previously had not touched, like "The Trolley Song" from "Meet Me in St. Louis."

"She was a knockout," a columnist rave, "scoring a

10-minute standing ovation from an audience heavily laced with show business legends."

On opening night, December 8, the auditorium was packed with friends, like makeup artist Kevyn Aucoin, Broadway star Nathan Lane, Mary Tyler Moore, Rosie O'Donnell, Rex Reed, Joan Rivers and Barbara Walters. Liza stepped out singing "If I Had You," from "The Clock," the second film on which Judy Garland had worked with Vincente Minnelli. Time reported that "her voice, if not the exuberant, no-holds-barred instrument it once was, can still curl stylishly around numbers like 'I Got Rhythm' and 'Baubles, Bangles and Beads.' "

Professional theater critics were kind but cautious. Typical of the reviews was Michael Lewittes's comment, titled "Liza's Fading Star," in the New York Daily News. Lewittes acknowledged that Liza's voice was richer and more powerful than it had been in recent years, but noted that "she still doesn't shine nearly as brightly as her sequined Bob Mackie costumes." He thought the show suffered from too many chorus numbers and complained that a handful of songs, including "By Myself," were performed by the five male singer/dancers while Liza wasn't even on stage.

The New York Post's Michael Reidel wrote, "Act One looked and felt like a television variety show from the mid-70s." But he acknowledged that Act Two was "much better, with Liza sending herself up in 'I'm Glad I'm Not Young Anymore' and melting hearts with a gorgeous rendition of 'Baubles, Bangles and Beads.' "

Liza's constant coughing and sipping water on stage

had at least one critic wondering if she'd even come back for the second act. And yet, when she did return, everyone had to admit she was in better form.

Addressing her battle with drugs and alcohol, Liza said, "If you have this disease, you have it. And it is a medical disease. You have to be so careful. It can get you down. But then it's your responsibility to get back up." And she was determined to do that.

And so the end of the year found Liza back on Broadway in her own show, on the wagon, and saying, "I've got a good life."

CHAPTER 11

Liza's close call

"Sometimes I didn't know where I was.
I imagined I was in California, when really
I was here in Fort Lauderdale."

L iza had intended "Minnelli on Minnelli" to have a limited Broadway run, so it was no surprise when it closed January 2, 2000. She still had ambitious plans for the show, however, including recording the cast album and taking the production on tour. She told friends, "I want my dad to be proud of me." So determined was she to prove that she was still a great performer, in 2000, she would come close to working herself into an early grave.

Ben Vereen was on his way to Tunisia when his phone rang and he was informed that the Drama League was honoring Liza Minnelli. There was no question that he had to postpone his plans to be in the Pierre Hotel ballroom that night.

It was January 21, and more than 400 guests had paid up to $900 a head to watch Vereen, Sam Harris,

Chita Rivera, Liz Smith and a band led by Billy Stritch salute their beloved Liza. Dame Edna Everage appeared via videotape and, tongue-in-cheek, made a startling confession of her own: she was actually Liza's mother.

Frank Giacomo of the New York Observer reported that in the middle of performing "Magic to Do," Vereen broke into a piano-punctuated patter in which he revealed that ever since meeting Liza, "My life has never been the same. I love this woman. I love this woman with all my heart. I love you for loving her."

In the middle of the song, Vereen shared a story about something Liza taught him.

"She joined me one day, and I was feeling bad that day. I had a matinee that day. And I said, 'I don't think I can make it. I'm too tired.'"

Vereen recalled that Liza just looked at him and said, "No, this is what we do. This is why we were placed here. So you must go forth and do that. Necessity is the mother of invention. The necessary things you need will be there when you step upon the boards."

With that, Vereen resumed the conclusion of "Magic to Do."

Vereen was followed by Dr. Ruth Westheimer, Chita Rivera and Sam Harris, who said that he and Liza both hailed from the Belter Belt where "less is — well, less."

For the finale, a valiant Liz Smith, wearing a white cowboy hat, boots and fringed Western wear, encouraged the audience to join her on the chorus as she launched into a new version of "Deep in the Heart of Texas." In this version, which she called "Deep in the Heart of Liza," there was room for Bob Fosse, sequins, Eloise, Vincente and Judy, Sid Luft and Lorna. Only John Simon was not allowed in the heart of Liza. The crowd went wild.

On February 29, the cast album of "Minnelli on Minnelli" was released on Angel Records, and Liza intended to take a pared-down version of the show on the road until fall. She was booked at San Francisco's Orpheum Theater for March 9-19, at Washington, D.C.'s, Kennedy Center April 12-16, and then in Chicago, Detroit, and Miami Beach in the fall.

Shortly before heading for San Francisco, Liza was interviewed at home by Chip Crews of the Washington Post. He admitted that his first sight of the new, plus-size Liza was a small shock. Not only was she considerably heavier, she walked with an uncertain tottery step.

Her 8th-floor apartment was like a museum of the 1970s. Nothing had changed there in the past 20 years. There were the four Warhol portraits in the foyer and, on a shelf nearby, the Oscar, Emmy, three Tonys and Golden Globes.

Liza was ebullient about taking the show on the road. "We have 17 cities booked. And that's only in this country. We're going overseas, we're going everywhere." She thought they might tour for the next two or three years.

"What's lovely is the way we tour, because we go out for two weeks. Then I come back . . . Because I'm a road rat. I know how to do this so you don't kill yourself. I tour nice and easy. You know, I take my pillows, I get there a couple of days early, I sing five shows and then I have two days off and then I sing again. I'm really — I'm well protected."

Liza assured Crews that she had been sober "almost two years" and attended AA meetings "every morning at 7 o'clock." As for following the same tragic path as her mother, Liza was still insisting that she was not Judy Garland. "The disease got her," she told Crews. "And I know it's a disease. She didn't. And there was no help. It was awful."

As for romance, Liza was not seeing anyone she was crazy about. "But I know lots of interesting men," she assured Crews. "And I like knowing a lot of interesting men. I'm finding it more interesting than just one." And in spite of all the losses in her life, she said, she still had Fred Ebb and John Kander to lean on.

Crews asked Liza what the biggest misconception about her was.

"That I'm weak," she answered. "You know what I mean? I'm a terribly strong woman who's come through all kinds of things."

From there Liza was on to San Francisco to unveil the new road-friendly version of "Minnelli on Minnelli." Still overweight, although she claimed to have shed 40 pounds, she also insisted that she was "like an ox." Some changes had been made in the Broadway show: arrangements were tweaked, dance numbers were added, and there was a new Bob Mackie costume for Liza.

For the first time, Liza talked about how close she had come to retiring. She revived the old country-living dream she had shared with Rex Kramer 30 years ago. She could see herself belting out the theme to "Green Acres" while working on her own farm. "If I hadn't gotten my voice back," she told a pal, "I'd have gotten a farm and spent my last days raising cairn terriers and standard poodles."

The success of "Minnelli on Minnelli" had convinced her to put off those plans for a few years.

"I've got my life together again — and my career," she added. "But I still want to make my dream of raising animals and growing things come true. I want to swap all my designer gowns for a pair of overalls. I want to forget all the greedy people. I want to be with my dogs and the other animals I intend to get. They're the only creatures you can really trust. I'll work until I'm 60, then it's off to the country to be a farmer. If you want to see me then, you'd better be prepared to put on a good pair of boots because I'll be enjoying life on the farm with my doggies."

On April 12, Liza presented the first of five "Minnelli on Minnelli" shows at the Kennedy Center Opera House in Washington, D.C. The reception was mixed. In one review, Megan Rosenfeld of the Washington Post admitted that the show "was neither as bad as I had feared nor as great as I had hoped." What troubled Rosenfeld was Liza's physical deterioration. She knew that she wasn't supposed to care that Liza was "as plump as a penguin," she wrote, especially since Liza herself made fun of her weight in witty new lyrics to "I'm Glad I'm Not Young Anymore." After all, didn't we all want to encourage rebellion against the unreal thinness we saw on TV? "But I do care," said Rosenfeld, "I care because she's so out of breath, and she's only 54."

Rosenfeld was also troubled by Liza's relentlessly positive spin on her chaotic childhood. She yearned for just a small hint that all was not paradise.

On Sunday, April 30, around 6 p.m., a frightened Liza was rushed to the emergency room of Johns Hopkins Hospital in Baltimore. She was as weak as a rag doll — hacking, coughing and gasping for air. Her voice was gravelly and she was wheezing. She was rushed to a special unit where aides administered oxygen and put her on a ventilator to help her breathe. Her blood oxygen level had dropped to a critical level. Liza was treated for double pneumonia. "She was in serious condition and for several hours her fate was in God's hands," said an insider. "No one knew if she was going to make it. Thank God she pulled through. She's on her way to making a complete recovery."

Liza was forced to cancel her tour. To her horror, she learned that she might end up in a wheelchair if she did not undergo another grueling round of hip replacement surgery and a spinal fusion. But doctors wouldn't do the surgery until she lost more than 60 pounds.

Liza showed immense resolve. "I'm feeling pretty bad. I ache terribly," Liza admitted. "But I'm determined not to let this get me down. I'm in pain and I need medical attention. I can't pretend I'm superwoman. I hate disappointing my audience, but I can't even walk, forget dancing! And my audience has been everything to me. Especially for this show. I came back for them. And for my dad."

Insiders blamed her collapse on overwork. "Liza was so determined to show the world she's still a great performer that she came close to working herself into an early grave," said an insider. "By October 1999, she'd lost 40 pounds on a high-protein diet and killer training program. Liza told me, 'I work all day with composers and voice coaches. I work with a physical trainer from 7 to 8 each morning. I go through my dance routines. I want my dad to be proud of me.' In the past few years Liza has endured knee and hip surgeries, suffered arthritis, battled depression, struggled with substance abuse and had polyps removed from her vocal cords. And she's bitterly disappointed that her comeback has been ruined. But stay tuned! Never-say-die Liza is sure to bounce back."

Liza went on a strict diet and by the end of the summer, she had lost a considerable amount of weight. She told a friend, "Once those last few pounds go, I'll be entering the hospital for the hip surgery. I just want to get this over. I'm not happy unless I'm performing."

"It looks like the surgery will be done this fall," her publicist, Michael Hartman, said. "She is a little apprehensive, but it's a necessary procedure and she's going ahead with it."

Liza retreated to a rented two-story ranch house in Fort Lauderdale. The $4,000-a-month waterfront home would soon become the setting for the greatest drama in her life.

The newest member of Liza's household was M'Hammed Soumayah. Once employed by the King of Morocco, M'hammed was Halston's assistant in 1979 and was with him when he died in 1980. Before he passed away, Halston had implored M'Hammed to "please take care of Liza." Now M'hammed Soumayah became Liza's constant companion, assistant, bodyguard and chauffeur.

M'Hammed was with Liza in early October while she rested at home in Fort Lauderdale, preparing for the hip replacement surgery. Although she had difficulty walking, restless Liza made the rounds of Fort Lauderdale clubs and restaurants in a wheelchair, accompanied by M'hammed.

Liza's next crisis began on Sunday afternoon, October 8. At 5 p.m., in the middle of singing with M'hammed, she suddenly collapsed. He immediately phoned 911 and told the operator, "A woman is having a heart attack. It is Liza Minnelli." A fire rescue unit and an engine company promptly responded to the call.

"We found her unconscious on the floor, disoriented and suffering what we believed was a stroke," said Chief Stephen McInerny. Liza was "babbling incoherently and suffering paralysis on one side of her body."

They gave her oxygen and an IV before paramedics sped her to the emergency entrance of the nearby Cleveland Clinic, where she was admitted under the name Elizabeth Nae.

Her ordeal was just beginning. "During the emergency treatment in the ambulance, Liza lapsed into a coma. She was in and out of the coma for several days." She was in such bad shape that the hospital wouldn't allow any visitors. The paramedics saved her life, but Liza's condition would be touch and go for several days.

Dr. Nestor Galvez and other ER doctors discovered that rather than a stroke, Liza was suffering from convulsions caused by the rare herpes encephalitis virus. On October 23, Dr. Maurice Hanson, a neurologist, disclosed that she was being treated for viral encephalitis. Staffers at the hospital were stunned by how ill she appeared. Said one, "Even veteran hospital workers who see tragedy and terrible suffering daily couldn't help but shed a tear for her."

Once doctors managed to stabilize Liza's condition, she was transferred to an acute care section on the hospital's third floor, where round-the-clock nurses attended to her in a private room.

At the Cleveland Clinic, caregivers gave Liza the VIP treatment, separating her from other intensive care patients and posting security guards at her door. Doctors would have to assess how much damage had been done to Liza's brain and body. For now, at least, she was in stable condition.

"Doctors were extremely concerned over Liza's condition," a close friend said. "The encephalitis was life-threatening, because it causes swelling of the brain. But she has other serious medical worries."

On October 16, doctors thought Liza had improved enough to go home, and she was quietly released late that afternoon. But just a few days later, severely dehydrated, she was rushed back to the hospital.

"Liza was in real bad shape," said a friend. "After intensive treatment she began to show a little improvement but doctors have told her that recovery will be slow. And they cannot guarantee she won't suffer permanent brain damage. Everyone is concerned she will be mentally impaired in some way. Liza would be devastated if she had to depend on others to take care of her."

Fortunately, Liza was bombarded with calls from well-wishers like Elizabeth Taylor. "Liz was very worried," said an insider. "But she managed to ease Liza's fears and calm her down."

The ordeal even helped patch up the long-running

feud between Liza and Lorna, who called to give her sister support, and soon flew to her side. The outpouring of love lifted Liza's spirits. They had disagreed over Liza's drug use, how to market their mother's name and Lorna's public criticism. Now, Liza was seen clinging to her sister with one hand, and giving a feeble wave with the other as Lorna pushed her wheelchair out of the hospital October 30.

As she was wheeled to a waiting white stretch limousine, Liza said bravely, "I feel wonderful. I'm with my sister and I've never felt better. I nearly died. It's so wonderful to be alive and with my sister."

Liza's spokesman, Michael Hartman, added, "Because of the severity of her illness, it will take several months for her to recover. She will need round-the-clock care.

The truce between Liza and Lorna barely lasted until mealtime. They soon started exchanging angry shots in a battle of the bulge. Once Liza got home, all she could think about was food. Lorna wanted her to dine sensibly on salads, but Liza was demanding her favorite calorie-packed foods.

"Lorna began lecturing her on how she should be eating light meals, salads and lean meats, but Liza would have none of it," explained a friend. "She just said, 'Lorna, I love you, but I'm going to eat what I want.' Lorna told her, 'Are you crazy? You can't be eating anything fattening. You need to lose weight for your upcoming hip operations.' And Liza roared back, 'Look who's talking! You're as big as a house! Who died and made you Jenny Craig?'"

The heat between the sisters died down when they got out of the kitchen and they had a chance to talk for the first time in years. More than once, they cried in each other's arms, apologizing for the past. But Lorna was still concerned about Liza's weight and desperately tried to convince her to eat sensibly.

A grateful Liza brought Lorna with her when she returned to the Cleveland Clinic Christmas party in December. She thanked the doctors, nurses and other staffers for saving her life. Wearing a pink jacket and black pants, Liza took to the stage and sang a song from "Cabaret," then gave a heartfelt speech that had her audience weeping. "Liza was totally charming," said one observer. "She thanked people individually and made it clear that she's very grateful for the terrific job they did."

Liza was still not completely recovered, however. During the emotional visit, she had to sit down for several minutes to gather her strength.

Once Liza was on the road to recovery, Neal Travis of the New York Post posed a question that was on the minds of many. What had Liza been doing in Fort Lauderdale, alone in a rented house, with no one but her houseman for company?

"Liza, a fragile figure at the best of times, has always kept a circle of friends around her," wrote Travis. His sources differed about what had happened to the people who had always been around Liza in the past. Some said that she had recently started discouraging her acquaintances from paying court to her.

"She went to Florida to get away from the regular crowd of hangers-on," wrote Travis. "She has traveled in a crowd for pretty well all her adult life, even if it has sometimes gotten in the way of a budding love affair. Peter Sellers suggested that she ditch her entourage. 'I can't do that, Peter,' she replied. 'They are my friends and they will always be with me.'"

Possibly Liza had realized that all the attention had not always been in her best interest. Now, facing a health crisis, she was putting herself first.

Her bout with encephalitis had been so debilitating, Liza said, that it left her totally disoriented. "Sometimes I didn't know where I was. I imagined I was in California when really I was here in Fort Lauderdale." As for Travis's question? Since she had left Johns Hopkins Hospital in April, she had not been "up to hanging out" with her showbiz chums.

Liza insisted she was not alone. Her manager, Gary Labriola, lived near the house she had rented, and her chauffeur and aide, M'Hammed Soumayah, was with her almost constantly. Her dog Lilli was also there, and she was in constant touch with her publicist, Michael Hartman, and her main assistant, Lisa Zay, in New York. Several friends had flown to visit her, including Jack Haley Jr., Charles Aznavour, Chita Rivera, Liz Rosenberg, John Kander and Fred Ebb. Others called regularly to check on her. Liza chose to go to Florida to get some sun, lose weight, rest and recuperate. She had been doing just that when her latest ailment struck.

She had overcome her illness, but little did she know that things were about to get worse. Soon Liza would be faced by a new and completely unexpected challenge.

CHAPTER 12

"You Are Not Alone"

"I'm clean, sober and fit for my new life."

Early in 2001, a new crisis loomed for Liza Minnelli — she was going broke. Her bout with encephalitis had forced her to postpone the second operation on her left hip. She hadn't worked since April, and she wouldn't be able to resume performing until she had her hip replacement surgery. She couldn't have the hip operation until she lost weight, but the longer she was inactive, the more she piled on the pounds.

Liza tried to stay calm, and she was able to put on a brave front, thanks in large part to her reconciliation with Lorna. But friends feared she was facing an uphill battle. Two years earlier, Liza had sold her house in Las Vegas for $2.1 million and that money was already gone.

Her production company had a payroll of $1 million a year. Wherever she toured, she traveled with a small army of musicians, grips and miscellaneous assistants. A lucky few of them traveled in first class with Liza. The rest flew business class. No one who traveled with Liza flew economy. Once, when a promoter questioned the expense, Liza grew stern. "You think that all these people who work like dogs for weeks and months on end, all over the country and the world, helping me do what I do, don't deserve to travel comfortably?"

Now Liza was forced to make drastic cuts and layoffs in the New York and Los Angeles offices. She considered selling the Beverly Hills house she had inherited from Vincente. Her stepmother still lived there. It was worth $2 million, but it was costing her a fortune in upkeep, and Liza's accountants told her that she could not afford it anymore.

"I'm scared. I'm definitely running out of money," she told a friend. "I can't continue like this much longer. If I don't get back to work soon, I don't know what I'll do."

Given her weight and poor physical condition, her friends doubted she would ever perform in public again, certainly not before she underwent more operations. "She needs another hip replacement, and that's going to be very painful for her," a friend confided. "It will be another long recovery period. Her hip is totally corroded. She can't bear any pressure on it now. And her knee is bothering her too."

Her hefty size caused new agony. Liza had gotten so big she couldn't walk more than a few feet. She depended on a wheelchair to get around. It seemed as if the only time Liza went out was to go to a restaurant, and when she wasn't eating out, she was eating in. She even had banana cream pies flown in from a favorite New York restaurant.

The nearly constant onslaught of troubles had left Liza very sad and depressed, but she still tried to strike an upbeat tone when a reporter found her lunching at a restaurant near her Fort Lauderdale home. It was one of her first outings since she had been felled by viral encephalitis.

"I'm trying to take it day by day, and every day it gets better," she said. "I'm trying to stay calm and be happy. I'm loving my home here in Florida and the company of my good friends," she added, pointing to her companions Rhonda and Jack Koussevitzky, local realtors, and her ever present bodyguard, M'Hammed.

Most of all, said Liza, she was grateful to have Lorna's help.

"My sister has been by my side throughout this ordeal. I don't know what I would have done without her. I've gotten such loving care, it's been extraordinary. I'm so lucky Lorna is back by my side."

On "Extra," Lorna told interviewer Leeza Gibbons about the reconciliation with Liza and described their relationship as "great. I think that when someone is sick, especially if you love that person, everything else doesn't matter anymore."

Liza was still too weak to travel. There was no way she could attend the Theater Hall of Fame Awards January 29. The people around her wouldn't allow it. She was in Florida, still facing back and hip surgery, still confined to a wheelchair.

Ever the contrarian, Liza did make a surprise appearance in New York at the Drama League's tribute to Chita Rivera at the Pierre Hotel February 5.

Dressed in a loose black tunic and tight black trousers, Liza drew the loudest applause at the dinner. She explained that she had "escaped from a hospital in Florida." She was unable to sing, but she read a telegram she had intended to send to her friend and colleague. "You changed my life. I promise you did, Chita," she declared in a hoarse, vibrant voice. When she finished, Liza walked slowly off the stage, leaning on the arm of a young man.

Liza stayed on in New York and for the next few weeks seemed to be everywhere, even at lawyer Mark Sandroff's "Night of 1000 Clients" birthday party at Laura Bella. "She partied. She drank. She wound up with alcohol poisoning two weeks later," a source revealed.

And once Liza fell off the wagon again, she began drinking more and more as she sank deeper and deeper into depression over her physical condition. She was hiding vodka bottles everywhere. One close friend threatened to end their relationship if Liza did not stop drinking.

"Liza, whether you want to believe it or not, you're dying," the friend warned her. "I'm not going to stand by and watch any longer while you commit suicide."

Liza had to hit bottom before she could start looking up again. She and her sister Lorna had set up a support system to make sure she stayed clean and sober. She insisted that she was dead serious this time, adding, "I know if I don't, I'm dead!"

A wheelchair-bound Liza faced another setback when she was hit with a series of painful migraine headaches and admitted to New York Hospital-Cornell Medical Center.

Frustrated and defeated, she said, "I'm looking forward to being out of pain. Thank goodness M'hammed, my wonderful houseman, got me to the hospital. My doctor said my neck was pinched and that was causing the migraines. My back, hip and neck are all related. I don't know exactly when I'll have the surgeries, but I'm going to be so much better when I get my hip and back operations."

Pals were praying for her recovery but feared that financial problems and stress might stand in the way. Liza so feared running out of money that she had been selling off cherished heirlooms from her mother. She contacted auction houses and even approached the online auction site eBay. Back in 1997, she had had the 200 gowns that Halston had designed for her, a one-of-a-kind collection, appraised at more than $1 million. Friends wondered if she planned to sell off them as well. Her auction plans took up so much time that Liza had already postponed a scheduled hip operation earlier that year.

"I don't know whether she is more afraid of running out of money or having another operation," added a friend. "She is always in a lot of pain after surgery — and painkillers are a 'no-no' for Liza."

Pals feared that her career might be over, but a cheerful and optimistic Liza assured her fans that she was headed for the comeback trail: "I can't wait to get back on stage!"

Nevertheless, she apparently needed another wakeup call. At New York Hospital, "Liza was about as close to dying as she could be," an insider revealed. "She was really in terrible shape. She has alcohol poisoning. They're taking aggressive measures to save her life."

Doctors were with her in the intensive care unit on a constant basis. They didn't know if she was going to live or die. Two huge bodyguards were posted at the door. The next day she had a stream of concerned visitors.

Liza's AA friends were called. They came to help her and were tough on her, too. They told her to stop feeling sorry for herself and get back into a rehab program. When her AA friends were around, Liza tried. Her belief that she would get back on stage again was all that kept her going. She was determined to make it.

Liza celebrated her 55th birthday at the Cornell Medical Center on March 12. The next day, she transferred to the Hospital for Special Surgery to have her left hip replaced. She was scheduled to undergo back surgery March 14; surgery to replace her left hip was scheduled to take place 10 days later. But first, doctors would conduct a week of tests and build up her immune system. During the tests, doctors discovered that she had life-threatening blood clots in her chest. They immediately canceled the hip and back surgeries and told Liza the blood clots would have to be her first priority.

Liza was devastated. Against her doctor's wishes, she checked herself out of the hospital and headed back to her New York apartment. She just could not deal with any more health problems.

After taking anticoagulants to break up the blood clots, Liza returned to the hospital for surgery. Finally, Liza's left hip was replaced March 21, 2001, at New York's Hospital for Special Surgery. But Liza's ordeal was not quite over. She was slow to shake off the anesthesia and began hallucinating.

Days after her hip surgery, Liza was rushed to Cornell Medical Center with alcohol poisoning again. As a crew brought her in, she was trying to speak to her dead father. Doctors feared she might be having another bout of encephalitis.

Physicians made plans to perform additional surgery on her back and knee as soon as two weeks after the hip replacement. Liza was eager to begin physical therapy and hoped to return to work by the end of the year.

While Liza was hospitalized, a visit from her old friend Ben Vereen had a better effect on her than any medicine her doctors could have prescribed. Ben had completely recovered from the serious injuries he suffered after he was hit by a truck nine years earlier. He inspired Liza so much that she was out of her bed and walking later that day.

As bighearted as ever, Liza took time off from battling health woes to praise the TV miniseries based on Lorna's book. "It was so inspiring," she said after watching ABC's two-part biographical drama, "Me and My Shadows." She was very moved by Judy Davis's performance in the role of Judy Garland. It reminded her of the many highs and lows in life. Liza wanted to get back to work. She could still sing magnificently. It was her physical health that was the problem.

"My mom was a talent in a billion," Liza said, after watching the movie. "But I believe that I've still got a lot to give, too."

With all Liza's health problems, few believed that she would turn up for her April tribute at the Sheraton Bal Harbour beach resort in Miami Beach. The benefit, for CenterOne, an AIDS charity, drew a mixed bag of performers, from Mickey Rooney to Aaliyah. But Liza did show up, in black caftan, receiving a standing ovation when she took the stage and sang "Maybe This Time." Jon Secada read a poem about Liza written by Chita Rivera. It included a reference to the Tin Man, and Liza quipped that her new hip made her "the Tin Woman."

At the time, David Gest was busy with his own tribute: a concert honoring his longtime friend, Michael Jackson. On April 17, David announced that "Michael Jackson: The Solo Years, 30th Anniversary Celebration" would be held at Madison Square Garden on Friday, September 7. He promised that Michael would perform duets with Whitney Houston, Britney Spears and other stars. Michael would also reunite for the evening with his brothers — Jackie, Jermaine, Marlon, Tito and Randy — and sing many of the Motown tunes that made the Jackson 5 famous. The concert would coincide with the September release of Jackson's long-awaited "Invincible" album.

By May 2001, Liza was so weak, physically and mentally, that friends feared she would not have the strength to deal with yet another crushing blow. Her former husband, Jack Haley Jr., was gravely ill.

Although they had been divorced for years, they had remained close friends. Jack was much more than an ex-husband to Liza. He had been her rock during her recent bad times. They spoke on the phone all the time. Liza was constantly telling friends how much she adored him.

Haley's health had deteriorated so drastically that he

was saying goodbye to his closest friends, including Liza. Ravaged by a combination of diabetes and liver and heart problems, he had been confined to a wheelchair for more than a year. Now he was losing circulation in his extremities. His body was simply shutting down. It was just a matter of time — and Liza was devastated.

No matter how bad she was feeling, Jack had always known what to say to make her feel better. And he never complained about his own health, which is why she was so surprised to hear how ill he was.

Liza was not well enough to travel from her Florida home to visit Haley in Los Angeles. Tearfully, she told a pal, "Jack has always been there for me — I hope I get the chance to be there for him."

Jack's assistant soon called Liza in New York to warn her that he was failing. She planned to fly to California, but Jack died of respiratory failure early Saturday morning, April 21, 2001, at UCLA Medical Center in Santa Monica. Hospital staffers summoned his former fiancee, Nancy Sinatra, who had left his bedside only hours before.

Liza was inconsolable. She issued a statement saying, "I fell in love with him the first time I met him, and I have loved him with all my heart ever since."

Liza had endured so much agony in the past six months that friends feared Jack's death would be the last straw. She had been drinking more and more as she sank deeper into depression over her physical condition. A pal revealed that "she was hiding vodka bottles all over the place."

"Liza is blaming herself for not being there," said a friend. "Once she starts blaming herself, she starts drinking and taking pills. My fear, and the fear of a lot of her friends is that one of these times she's not going to come out of it."

At least she now had Lorna back in her life. Her reconciliation with her sister continued to be a source of solace for Liza. Late in May, Liza even made an unannounced trip out to the eastern end of Long Island to catch Lorna's Judy Garland tribute show for the first time. Liza showed up alone and slipped quietly into the Westhampton Beach Performing Arts Center.

At one point, Lorna stopped the show and announced, "My very best friend is here — Liza Minnelli!" Liza stood and the audience applauded wildly.

"It was great — just a wonderful moment," Lorna said later. "The past is all behind us, and we are getting along wonderfully, like two sisters should."

For those who thought it would never last, Lorna said, "We need each other. It was great to be able to demonstrate in public the bonds between us. I couldn't be happier."

Around this time, Michael Jackson suggested to David Gest that he add Liza Minnelli to the roster of stars for the planned September concert. Gest was dubious, but Jackson insisted, "I want Liza in it." He had heard all the stories about Liza's problems over the last few years.

Gest finally sent his musical director, Joey Melotti, to hear Liza sing a few numbers. Melotti didn't even wait to get back to David. He called him from Liza's home. She could hear him assure David, "Yeah, three octaves! I'm telling you, she's got her voice back. You've gotta come down here and hear this."

So he did.

When he heard her, Gest immediately added her to the bill.

That summer, many industry insiders doubted that a Michael Jackson reunion concert could happen. Two Jackson brothers were already publicly complaining. They feared that the top ticket price of $2,500 put them out of reach of their fan base.

"The exorbitant ticket prices being charged by the promoters will prevent some of our most loyal and true fans from attending the shows," Jermaine and Randy Jackson stated in a letter they circulated to the media in late July. "Further, it is almost embarrassing that no charities have been named to benefit from this momentous occasion."

Gest fired back with a statement of his own: the Jacksons "will reunite without Jermaine." The same day he announced that Liza had joined the all-star salute to the King of Pop as a co-chair of the event. Accompanied by a 300-member gospel choir, Liza would perform Michael Jackson's "You Are Not Alone."

In August, *NSYNC backed out, citing a conflict with rehearsals for the MTV Awards. "*NSYNC will not have time to rehearse the 'Dancing Machine' number with the Jacksons in the way Michael planned to present it," Gest said in yet another statement. "Michael looks forward to working with *NSYNC in the future, as he is a very big fan of the group."

He may have lost one boy band, but Gest still had Britney Spears, Destiny's Child, Ray Charles, and, of course, Liza. The list of stars committed to the event was growing, and he had just added 50 "Leading Ladies of the Silver Screen," a bevy of beauties that included Angie Dickinson and Patty Duke.

The most important star he had landed was Liza, who fell head over heels for the 46-year-old producer almost immediately.

"It was love at first sight," revealed a friend of Liza. "She told me, 'I've never met anyone like David before. We just clicked right away. We have so many friends in common that I'm surprised we never got together before. And with David being a producer, I'm thinking about getting back on stage and performing. I feel like I'm living in a dream. I have a reason to sing again.'"

By opening night, they were living together, alternating between David's West Side apartment and Liza's longtime East Side home. When the two fell in love in late 2001, she was close to her all-time high of 200 pounds, hooked on booze and pills and in poor health. Now Liza seemed to have a new energy.

September 7 was the first of the two big nights, and Liza admitted that she was shaky. "I felt like I was between a rock and a hard place," she said later. "Remember who you are," David told her. She was facing a large audience for the first time in months. Her hair had grown out and her body was hidden by a black and silver beaded caftan. Vanity Fair writer Jonathan Van Meter described her struggle to get through "You Are Not Alone": "Her voice — always a singularly odd and unpredictable instrument — seemed incapable of going where she wanted it."

The show proved to be the perfect New Millennium

version of the great variety productions that Judy Garland had known in vaudeville and that Vincente Minnelli had grown up in with in the Minnelli Brothers Traveling Circus. Liza herself had made her earliest TV appearances on variety shows like the "Ed Sullivan Show.'"

When Liza left the stage after a standing ovation, David Gest was relieved and pleased. About three days earlier, he had sensed that Liza might have a problem. Two days before and the day of the show she was fine. Tonight, Liza had given what he considered a brilliant performance. After the show, they celebrated with a big party at Liza's. There he sensed that all the pressure was catching up with her, "because she felt that maybe she needed a drink or something to keep up."

During rehearsals Liza would frequently raise her hand, saying, "I think I'm going to drink. I got to get some help."

The second show was Monday, September 10, and the California group, which included Marlon Brando, Elizabeth Taylor, Corey Feldman and Michael Jackson himself, prepared to go home the next day.

Early on the morning of Tuesday, September 11, as the performers were still sleeping off their last night at the Garden, word reached them that two planes had flown into the World Trade Center. There was panic in the hotel, as Corey Feldman has described it. Michael Jackson arranged limousines to get Liz Taylor and Marlon Brando out of town, since the airports were shut down.

As news of the terrorist attack spread, Liza learned that the sister of one of her oldest friends had been aboard the first plane that crashed into the World

Trade Center. Berry Berenson Perkins, the kid sister of Liza's best friend, Marisa Berenson, and a tomboy whom Liza had helped match up with Tony Perkins many years ago, had been aboard the plane. She was returning from a home she owned on Martha's Vineyard, where she had been completing work on her contribution to a book about Halston. Everyone in Liza's life was connected, and now David was, too. We can only speculate that the success of the concert, followed by the horror of September 11, and the tragic news that Berry had become a casualty clinched the love that had been growing between Liza and David.

For weeks the city reeled from the attack, under the leadership of Mayor Rudolph Giuliani.

On Friday, September 21, baseball returned to New York for the first time since the attack. Mayor Giuliani, Diana Ross, Marc Anthony and bagpipers took part in a moving tribute. Wearing an FDNY sweatshirt and a cap with the NYPD shield, Giuliani was cheered by Mets and Braves alike.

"This is the way life gets back to normalcy," said Giuliani. "You can't just concentrate on the tragedy. It's so wonderful that those people have such confidence to turn out in such large numbers. Things will be back to normal when I hear boos at Shea Stadium," said New York's most famous Yankees fan.

At the seventh-inning stretch, Liza stepped out onto the field to sing "New York, New York." She was joined by the crowd and hugged Mets hitter Jay Payton.

"I'm so happy to be here," she said.

Later in September, it was reported that Liza had

"miraculously thrown her walking cane away." She planned to perform at the Thalians annual ball, this year a star-studded tribute to Jack Haley Jr. to be held October 13 at the Century Plaza Hotel in Los Angeles. "Liza is training like an Olympian so she'll be in tip-top shape for her big comeback," said a pal. "She's dropped more than 20 pounds, and she's walking every day. She wants the world to know she's back — and feeling better than ever."

Unfortunately, Liza did not make it to the Thalians 46th Annual. A last-minute change of plans kept her from headlining the show as promised. The event, which drew more than 800 guests and raised $400,000, did include performances by Debbie Reynolds, Connie Stevens and more. Nancy Sinatra served as honorary chair. A few days later, the word through the grapevine was that "Debbie Reynolds is not happy with Liza Minnelli. The story going around Los Angeles is that Minnelli fears flying at this sensitive time and sources claim organizers of the event learned of the cancellation from Delta Airlines."

Liza's New York representative, Michael Hartman, acknowledged that she had canceled the trip, but countered, "She had something to do in New York that week. And when the president and FBI issued warnings and alerts, she realized she didn't want to be stuck out of town." Hartman also insisted that Liza had called the Thalians to cancel "days before the event."

In November, David brought her to the roof of his building and proposed. She had lots of reasons for saying no, but she found herself saying yes. From then on, the couple could not stop celebrating. They were spotted at the nightclub One51, where Liza danced hip-hop in the club's VIP room until 1 a.m. A week later, she and David hosted an engagement party with 100 guests at her apartment.

In mid-December Liza was so overwhelmed by paparazzi as she was leaving John Barrett's salon at Bergdorf-Goodman that she waited in the store's security offices until things calmed down. "This place is marvelous," she said. "I must come back." Liza was so rattled by the photographers that she didn't seem to remember that she was a regular at John Barrett or that she had once filmed a scene for "Arthur" there. A few days later, Liza and David were seen with models Marcus Schenkenberg and Carmen listening to DJ Stretch Armstrong spinning at the Tribeca Grand.

Liza also revealed that she wanted to get married at St. Patrick's Cathedral in a gown with a train "a mile long" and to adopt four kids. "David is used to putting on large events," said a pal, "so their wedding ceremony should really be spectacular."

David was busy producing "Miracle on 34th Street," his yearly Christmas extravaganza at Madison Square Garden. But he was not too busy to notice that Liza needed help.

Just before Christmas, Liza secretly checked herself into the Caron Foundation rehabilitation center in Wernersville, Penn. The center charges about $30,000 for a 28-day stay. She emerged booze and drug free and 20 pounds lighter. Soon, more pounds would melt off.

Gest said later, "It was a very lonely, lonely Christmas and a very lonely New Year because you know you have to say to people, well she's here, well she's there. And then the tabloids of course found out, and they were kind, this time, they were kind."

Even though Liza had plenty of emotional support, spending the holidays in rehab was very difficult for her. But her drug problem had gotten so out of control that she couldn't put it off another day. In the beginning, Liza was reserved and kept mostly to herself. She wandered around the grounds alone, cried a lot, and wouldn't eat. As the days passed, she opened up to the other patients and started making friends. When she began attending group sessions and talking about her drug use, everyone noticed a huge change in her personality. Liza said that her fiance, David, helped inspire her to get clean again because he was so concerned for her life. She blamed drugs and alcohol for her previous failed relationships, and she didn't want their marriage to turn out to be another disaster. She vowed not to let that happen.

"Every time Liza spoke about David," said a source, "her eyes filled with tears, and she expressed how grateful she was that he stood by her side through this difficult time. He visited her regularly while she was at Caron."

David had also reluctantly taken over managing Liza's career. "I never wanted to be her manager," he said. "I just know what's best for her. I will never let my wife be taken advantage of by anybody. There are too many sharks out there."

"And I've met them all," laughed Liza.

Liza shed more pounds in rehab and followed a regimen of exercise and dance routines. She credited her renewed vigor to David Gest.

"She's doing everything she can to get herself back

into shape. She wants to show the world she can do it," Gest said.

Liza assured her friends — and David — that she was going to make it this time.

"I feel great," she told one insider. "This is the best thing I've done for myself in ten years."

Liza surprised patrons at the Bergdorf-Goodman beauty salon when she flashed a stunning 3.5-carat diamond ring and gushed, "I'm so happy!"

But not all of Liza's friends were pleased with her latest move. News of her engagement upset many of them, who feared that she would get hurt.

"I've pleaded with Liza not to marry this guy. If she does, it will be the worst decision of her life," one friend confided to the press. "For the moment, Liza believes she really is in love, but none of her friends think this relationship will last. I told her, 'You want to be friends with the guy, go ahead, be friends, you don't have to marry him.'"

Some were troubled by his appearance. "David is a man addicted to plastic surgery," one complained, "and most recently had his nose resculpted to make himself look like his good pal Michael Jackson." Others likened Gest's look to David Geffen, the gay music mogul who had been a close friend of Cher's. Another insider detailed Gest's obsession with the onetime child star Shirley Temple. An entire section of his West Side apartment was devoted to his collection of Shirley Temple memorabilia. Some people who'd seen it called it "a shrine."

And what about Lilli, the cairn terrier who had been Liza's constant companion through all her ordeals since the breakup of her marriage to Mark

Gero? Could a lifelong animal lover find happiness with a man who evicted a puppy from his building and insisted that all pets be muzzled?

After all that Liza had been through, her friends wanted her to be happy. But was David Gest the man to make her happy?

Everybody was a little shocked," Lorna acknowledged. "But she sounded very happy when she invited me to the wedding."

CHAPTER 13

Liza Minnelli – happy at last

"I'm in constant change now every day, because I realize I have a choice. I don't have to be a slave to anything."

At the beginning of 2002, David and Liza began planning the most glamorous, most joyous, and most publicized wedding that New York had seen in years. It was David's idea to have their reception at the Regent Wall Street just a few blocks from Ground Zero. Describing her lover's thinking as "strange and wonderful," Liza explained to the London Telegraph that "he thinks that it's time for people to go back downtown again without being frightened. To repossess the financial district."

Early in January, a lucky few hundred received invitations from Liza and David inviting them "to share the beginning of our new life together when we exchange vows Saturday, March 16."

When people asked Liza why they just didn't live together, she replied, "But we've been doing that. It's so different this time. I really waited a long time. And I thought I'd never get married again. And he thought he would never get married."

Invitees ranged from 3 1/2-year-old Spencer Hoge, son of ABC's Cynthia McFadden, to 80-something icons like Carol Channing and Mickey Rooney. This prompted one columnist to quip, "The guest list is from three to eternity." It was also revealed, that true to the Hollywood tradition, the happy couple had also hammered out a prenuptial agreement.

From the start, rumors and controversy surrounded the big event. In January the New York Post's Page Six reported that Elizabeth Taylor was demanding a private plane and luxury accommodations for herself and her entourage, who included a hairdresser, masseuse and secretary.

There was some confusion when Liza announced that the ceremony would be at St. Patrick's Cathedral. Someone pointed out that this might be awkward, since neither the bride nor groom was Catholic. Soon Liza announced that the ceremony would be moved a few blocks south to the Marble Collegiate Church at Fifth Avenue and 29th Street. The church was the home of the late Norman Vincent Peale, the man who preached "the power of positive thinking."

Despite the religious confusion, the happy couple planned to celebrate their union in front of 1,000 guests, including Elizabeth Taylor, Michael Jackson, Whitney Houston and Tony Bennett.

"This will be a once-in-a-lifetime party," Gest promised. "The reception will probably turn into an elegant jam session for about eight hours."

Since her brush with death from encephalitis, Liza

had grown closer to both of her sisters. She complained that many times when she visited Tina Nina and her two children in Mexico, where Tina Nina works with the Catholic Church, she would read that she'd been drunk somewhere in some club.

A new Liza was on parade. Gaining a fiance had helped Liza lose an amazing 80 pounds. Gest's love and a March 16 wedding date had convinced her to change her eating habits and start exercising. The results were miraculous. "It's like she's got a brand-new body," declared one pal. "She looks great. She's wearing fashionable clothes again and looks like the sexy Liza from her 'Cabaret' days. She's going to make a beautiful bride."

Gest had forbidden chocoholic Liza from indulging in sweets soon after they met, but her weight loss kicked into high gear when David put her on a high-protein diet.

"Liza has been eating healthy for months," said Anna Coste, manager of Vince and Eddie's, a Manhattan eatery where Liza is a regular. "She used to always have dessert, but now she orders a dinner of chicken, fish or salad — and that's it."

Liza was so excited about her wedding that she turned her life around. She was even planning to go on a European tour in the spring.

"She couldn't have done it without David," said a friend. "He's been encouraging and supporting her every step of the way. Liza is in love and happier than she's been in years."

Still, there were occasional signs of the old Liza. She gave a strange interview to the London Telegraph in which she described visiting Ground Zero and encountering Ben Vereen walking in the ruins. "He was holding a human hand. Just a hand!"

The New York Post's Page Six, never the most supportive of Liza, wondered why Vereen would pick up a body part at a crime scene and checked with Vereen's manager, Trevor Baptiste, who blamed the Telegraph. "Liza would never make such a statement that is so patently, blatantly false," he assured Page Six's Ian Spiegelman. He added, "The only reason I'm calling you back is because of the dear friendship between Ben Vereen and Liza Minnelli."

Liza also told the Telegraph, "I'm in constant change now every day because I realize I have a choice. I don't have to be a slave to anything."

In February, Larry King and his wife, Shawn, hosted a party for the engaged couple at the Sky Bar of the Mondrian Hotel in West Hollywood. The nearly 200 guests, including many of Hollywood's old elite, Nancy Sinatra, Loni Anderson and Sally Kirkland, dined and danced under a transparent tent raised over the Sky Bar's outdoor pool.

Liza and David held hands and kissed during dinner before Liza jumped on stage and belted out "New York, New York" and other signature hits.

"David and I are ideal for each other," she told friends at the affair.

As for her groom-to-be, he could not wait to tie the knot. "I know Liza has had three husbands," he said, "but I'm FOUR-ever!"

"David and Liza were glued to each other throughout the evening," said one guest. "They circulated together, greeting old friends and new with arms around each other, often hugging and kissing."

David told one friend, "I am so much in love with Liza! She's the best thing that's ever happened to me. She's my soul mate."

Denise Rich was to give the bridal shower luncheon on Wednesday, March 13, but it was suddenly canceled. Liz Smith reported that "Liza was offered a private gig in Short Hills, N.J., and believe me, the money for about four songs would go a long way toward alleviating the national debt."

Liz also reported that she had taken the engaged couple to see her friend Elaine Stritch in her one-woman show on Broadway. "It's certainly worth the pesky paparazzi to see those two lovebirds in public," she gushed. "Liza had lost so much weight she was back to her original youthful self. That didn't keep the couple from plunging into a big lobster-shrimp-seafood platter at Sardi's after the show." She added, "The Diet Coke flowed like wine."

Liz went home at 1 a.m. but David and Liza "continued on to Ashford & Simpson's Sugar Bar on 72nd Street, where Liza sang and won standing ovations."

On March 8, the smiling couple applied for their marriage license at New York's Municipal Building, near City Hall, where they received VIP treatment. They were escorted by three security officers past long lines and ushered into a VIP room to receive the certificate privately. New York State requires the couple to apply in person and pay $30. The Post reported that after 30 minutes, a chipper Liza, looking understated in a black overcoat decorated with an American flag brooch, emerged exclaiming, "We feel great," as they discreetly exited through a side door.

The Sunday before her wedding day, Liza was spotted at Marble Collegiate Church among those attending a service called "Celebrating the Spirit of Adoption," feeding rumors that she and David planned to start a family as soon as possible.

On March 12, Liza turned 56, and David gave her an aquamarine, gold and diamond ring to mark the occasion.

Although Liza and Lorna had publicly reconciled, and Lorna attended the California parties, she planned to be in Australia on Liza's big day. However, Page Six reported that Lorna was privately telling pals: "Are you kidding? I wouldn't go to that freak's wedding!" Page Six was uncertain whether she was referring to Liza or David.

Just days before the wedding, some guests canceled when they learned that David had sold rights to cover the event to OK! magazine. Whitney Houston, who was to sing "The Greatest Love of All," backed out on Thursday. She sent word from Miami that she was too busy completing her new album for Arista.

But pals confided that Whitney was "wary of being splashed all over the tabloids again and was especially disappointed" when what she thought was a small, personal appearance was billed in the press as "a star turn."

"Whitney had offered to sing for her friends Liza and David," the friend said. "She thought it would be a small, personal gift. But then it turned into this big, huge event. It turned into a professional gig and she just didn't want to do it."

None of the criticism bothered Liza. "David brought me back from the brink of death," she told friends. "No drink, no drugs for the past three months. He won't tolerate it."

For her first wedding to Peter Allen, Liza had worn ecru antique lace; for her second wedding to Jack Haley Jr., she wore a yellow pantsuit; and for her third, she had worn a pink chiffon cocktail dress. To those who questioned her choice of white for her fourth wedding, she said, "Listen, I know plenty of non-virgins who wear white. The gown's gorgeous and I've lost so much weight. I was 200 pounds. I'm now down to 120."

As for Whitney's sudden cancellation, "The total she demanded for singing one song at the wedding came to over $100,000," said one insider. There were rumors that Whitney was the only invited guest who was demanding sky-high perks. She was said to have asked for a private plane (costing at least $25,000) and hotels, limos and security — but when she wanted $25,000 for a dress, it was too much. David refused to comment. His associates assured, "He did not pay one dime to anyone to appear at this wedding or to sing at this party."

Whatever the rumors, Elizabeth Taylor managed to arrange to borrow her own private plane.

"When Natalie Cole was asked to stand in for Whitney Houston, she refused even to let others pay to fly her up from Nashville," Liz Smith reported. "She came on her own. Participation in this wedding was a gift to Liza."

Liza had a special reason for choosing each of her 13 bridesmaids, even one she had only known a few months. English actress and singer Martine McCutcheon had battled the same alcohol and health problems that Liza had. The 26-year-old performer was starring in the "East Enders" at age 18, and at 24, was starring in a revival of "My Fair Lady" in London. When vocal problems shattered her confidence, she sought comfort in alcohol. Liza met Martine when David read reviews of her show, heard her album and said to Liza, "You've got to meet this girl."

Martine said of Liza, "She took me under her wing from the minute she met me. When she first asked me to be her bridesmaid I thought she was joking. I told her, 'I can't be your bridesmaid, people have known you for years, I've known you for months. I'm worried you might think I'm something I'm not.'"

"What do you think I am, a sucker?" Liza replied. "Do you think I haven't been around a bit? Do you think I don't know a good person when I see one?"

"She gives me advice because she is someone who has been there and she is a survivor," explained Martine. "I think Liza sees something of herself in me. I think she knows that we have personality traits that are the same. We are very tough and very strong but we are also very vulnerable. As a result we have to take extra care of ourselves."

Liza tells Martine, "At the end of the day, you are human; do your job and go home."

Liza and David had barely begun married life when they were rocked by rumors that David is gay. Elton John's jokes on their wedding day had been hurtful enough. When he was asked what he would give Liza as a wedding gift, Elton brought down the house with the reply, "a heterosexual husband." Elton's spokesperson said, "It was just Elton fooling around."

Four days after the nuptials, on March 20, Liza and

David appeared on Larry King Live. When King brought up "the talk about your sexuality and the like," Gest replied vaguely, "I know who I am. That's the important thing. She knows who she is and we're so in love we've got our own world."

Michael Musto, columnist for the Village Voice was not convinced. "When Gest told Larry, 'I know who I am' and 'She knows who she is,' it made me wonder — ah, but does she know who HE is? Let's face it, Liza traditionally has not had the best 'gay-dar.'"

Rumors that David was gay were all over New York. "There is something very strange about David Gest," one close friend of Liza quipped.

That April the situation worsened when a disgruntled former girlfriend, Ruth Warrick, 86-year-old star of "All My Children," claimed that David had dated her for 15 years so he could appear to be heterosexual.

"If Liza was expecting passion with David on her wedding night, believe me, she's still waiting," said the four-times-wed Warrick. "David's been secretly into men, not women, for the entire twenty-five years I've known him!"

Warrick insisted that she needed no "gay-dar" to recognize Gest's sexual preference when they first met in Los Angeles in the late 1970s. "David was producing celebrity galas at the time and because he was bossy, demanding, temperamental and never seemed to have a girlfriend, even his own people called him 'a snippy little queen' behind his back. He walked and talked in a manner that people called 'swish.'"

Gest made such an effort to impress women that at first, Warrick said, she thought he was bisexual. But, she said, after they became close she concluded that he felt no attraction to women. "David didn't relate to me on a sexual level at all and I came to believe that he had never known passion with a woman," said Warrick.

"It never once occurred to me in twenty-five years that David was anything but a closet homosexual who for business and social reasons didn't want it known."

During all their years of dating, Warrick had never once seen him in the company of a "significant other" of either gender.

"He'd say, 'I don't have time for a love life,'" Warrick recalled, "and I'd say, 'Oh, I think you do, David — a very secret one.' He'd just laugh and say, 'No one can know for sure what I am unless they're in the bedroom with me.' I took that to mean that he had boyfriends on the side that he kept out of sight."

Warrick claimed that a desperate Gest had begged her to marry him five years ago, just to quash growing rumors that he was gay. "I turned him down," she recalled. "I told him, 'Marrying this old broad won't change the way people see you. Everyone is convinced that you're gay. I know it and you know it, so you might as well admit it!'"

According to Warrick, they were on vacation in Hawaii when Gest stunned her with his marriage proposal. She thought he was joking. "Finally he admitted, 'I need to be married.' He said, 'People are talking. Marriage is the answer.' He wanted a wife and as long as she was elegant, in showbiz, looked good on his arm and knew the score, he didn't much mind who she was."

Some insiders found Gest totally unconvincing as a heterosexual. "David adores Liza and has done wonders for her," said one pal. "But I wish he'd quit the big act, making up stories about being straight and having sex with Liza. Nobody who knows David Gest buys that. He looks gay, acts gay and talks gay. It's not a big deal among those who know him, but for reasons only he knows, David persists in acting heterosexual."

Gest's representative, Warren Cowan, insisted that his client was 100 percent heterosexual.

Did it really matter? Other longtime pals believed that Liza finally found what she wants in David. "At this point in her life, Liza's not necessarily looking for a sex life," said one. "In David she's found companionship, security and a lot of genuine love. For years she was the loneliest person I've ever known. With David she's found a protector and an admirer, which is exactly what she needs."

Some friends still had their doubts. "The horrible truth is that she's definitely married the wrong man for her — or any woman."

"David is a mercurial dazzler, a schmoozer and hustler who's the life and soul of every party," added another friend. "But husband material, he's definitely not."

The newlyweds temporarily postponed their honeymoon in Thailand and, after a brief rest in New York, headed for London to promote Liza's upcoming concert at Albert Hall. Things got off to a shaky start as she and David sat inside their limousine after taping a TV show. Thieves reached through her open window and tried to snatch the crystal cross she was wearing around her neck. Ten days later, she made a triumphant return to the stage.

David drove staffers at London's Lanesborough

Hotel nuts by demanding that the sheets be changed three times a day and the bathroom cleaned 10 times a day. When the germaphobe producer wasn't around to bark orders to the person on duty, Liza was more than happy to take over. "As far as she's concerned, whatever David says is gospel," said an insider. "Liza's becoming his mimic."

Rosie O'Donnell's final TV show marked not only the end of her talk show career but the abrupt end of her friendship with Liza. Rosie had been thrilled when Liza agreed to sing "Over the Rainbow" for the first time in public. The hope was for Rosie to end her show on a classic TV moment like Bette Midler singing "One for My Baby" to Johnny Carson on his last show.

But Liza wanted to sing a song called "Never Never Land" which ends with about six bars of "Over the Rainbow." This wasn't acceptable to Rosie. Liza suddenly discovered a scheduling conflict and bowed out.

Rosie told pals that Liza backed out of performing on her final show because Rosie was gay.

"Rosie is livid," a source confided. "She believes Liza canceled because Rosie recently came out as a lesbian and Liza feared that an appearance on Rosie's show would renew rumors that her new husband is gay. Liza committed to the show months ago, before Rosie announced that she was gay. At the time, Liza seemed very enthusiastic about helping Rosie go out with a bang."

Since then, however, Liza had married David, and the rumors about his sexuality were so widespread that an obviously hurt Liza stated publicly that she and Gest had an active sex life.

"Rosie is really PO'd," divulged one insider. "She believes Liza was worried the public would believe that her husband was gay if Liza went on the show of an openly gay person. And 'Over the Rainbow' is a favorite torch song of drag queens everywhere. Rosie thinks the association, with so much gayness, caused Liza to cancel. Rosie says she doesn't want or need friends who treat her differently because she's gay."

Liza's publicist chalked up her cancellation to "creative disagreements." But Rosie became even more infuriated when Liza showed up on "The View" — a show that Rosie considered competition. "Rosie doesn't think it's a coincidence that the five women on 'The View' are card-carrying heterosexuals," said the source. "She is very, very upset. It's a shame, because Rosie and Liza had been close for years and now their friendship is over."

That summer, Rosie was angrier than ever when she returned to standup comedy at the Mohegan Sun casino in Uncasville, Conn. She told a shocked audience: "I can say what I want. The bitch ain't so nice anymore."

The former "Queen of Nice" blasted a dozen top stars, and lashed out at Oprah, Joan Rivers and Michael Jackson. But she saved special vitriol for Liza. Rosie had been a guest at Liza's wedding celebration, but now she dismissed it as "the gayest thing since my last show." She said she saw Michael Jackson at the wedding but refused to speak to him. "I make it a rule not speak to pedophiles," she said, referring to the 1994 scandal when the pop star paid $40 million to a boy who claimed Jackson had molested him.

A reporter once asked Liza why she has been attracted to so many gay men. "Well, who else is in the theatre? Know what I mean?" she answered. "Are you going to meet a lot of basketball players when you're performing on Broadway? I think not."

How had Liza inherited her mother's status as a gay icon? "There is a difference in the genes with gay people," said Liza. "I find that gay people relate to women like me because I'm sensitive like they are. I describe what they are going through."

Liza's London concerts hit a sour note with fans and critics when she was caught lip-synching on stage. As far back as "The Act," Liza had experimented with lip-synching some of her songs during strenuous dance numbers. Ron Higgin, an assistant to David Gest, confirmed that Liza mimed several numbers at Royal Albert Hall. "She does lip-synch a couple of songs, but they are only her dance numbers," he admitted.

Another concertgoer noticed that Liza's lip-synching didn't seem to bother her audience. "They gave her a standing ovation just for surviving and showing up. Her new husband David sat in the front row wearing dark glasses and was on his feet with everybody else."

Liza had the last laugh when she made a spectacular stage comeback in London and credited her success to a great sex life. She won rave reviews for her new show, "Liza's Back," produced and directed by David Gest. She had so much energy she was dancing hip-hop in her shows. With her voice and figure back, Liza demonstrated her old form, inspiring standing ovations and as many as 14 encores a night. She received accolades from entertainment royalty like Sir

Andrew Lloyd Webber, Vanessa Redgrave, Sir Cliff Richard, Joan Collins, Sir Tim Rice, Sir John Mills and Petula Clark. They all called it one of the greatest stage performances they'd ever seen.

"Liza's Back" was so well received in London that David began making plans to bring the show to New York. They would open May 31 at the Beacon Theater. Then she wanted to take it on tour across Europe and the U.S., resume her film career and write a book or two.

She looked great, sounded great, and credited David Gest for her revitalized career.

"I have a husband who loves me in every way a woman dreams of being loved," Liza said in an interview that May. "We have the best sex ever. It makes me feel alive. My wedding night was special," Liza continued. "I was still a nervous bride, but David was a caring and tender lover. We have the most delightful sex life."

Gest added, "Our marriage is wonderful for both of us. It's all about love."

On top of all her entertainment plans, the 56-year-old entertainer revealed that she planned to adopt four children. "David and I want to complete our family with children to love. We both love children and believe in adoption. This is what we will do."

After years of pain and suffering from health woes, Liza had feared she might never entertain again. But now she had turned her life around with physical therapy, a healthy diet and a loving relationship with Gest. She credited her rapid weight loss to strict diet and exercise. "I eat lots of fruits and vegetables and Slim-Fast. I also went back to classes for dancing and worked my butt off — literally. David and I have a minimum two-hour workout each day. We also walk a mile during the early evenings."

Liza denied rumors that she had liposuction treatments. "No. Absolutely false. After all I've been through, I could have never survived liposuction." She also said that she would never again take the pain pills she found so necessary following her surgeries.

"I can't take them because I am a recovering alcoholic who is trying to help other alcoholics."

What's next for Liza? On her long list of plans is the revival of her old show "Minnelli on Minnelli," the tribute to her father she was forced to cut short in 1999.

"I would love to do 'Minnelli on Minnelli,' with David's input as producer. I respected my father and loved him with all my heart. I want his memory and works to always be remembered." Liza added, "I am so grateful to my fans for standing by me. I love life and wake up each day smiling. I am no longer afraid to look in the mirror."

But Liza was not changing her style for anyone. When a makeup artist suggested that she tone down her look — spiked hair, false eyelashes and lots of lipstick — she replied, "No. Give the people what they want!"

In June, Liza and David were reported to be talking to publishers about a pair of books. The first would be an autobiography detailing Liza's struggles with alcoholism and drug abuse, her financial woes, the life and death of her mother, her estrangement from Lorna and her wild times at Studio 54. The other book would be about health and fitness and would be jointly written with David, who had helped her lose 100 pounds.

David had given Liza things she never thought she would have again: a revitalized career, a man who loved her and a happy, healthy outlook on life. Only one thing was lacking: a child of her own.

Late in June, while vacationing in the south of France, Liza announced that they had begun procedures to adopt a child. "Liza and David can't wait," a friend revealed. "They've accomplished so much professionally. Now the goal is to have their own little bundle of joy."

Their decision to ultimately adopt four children did not surprise her stepmother, Lee Anderson Minnelli. Lee revealed that Liza has dreamed of having children "for as long as I can remember. I'm sure that Liza and David will make wonderful parents."

On September 3, Liza and David announced they were adopting a 3-year-old girl they called Serena, who would be joining their household in January.

"It just seems to me that with all the things I've learned and that my parents taught me, it's time to pass something on. And David has made that possible," Liza said. "This baby is the most important thing to us. Our obligation as parents will come first and foremost before anything else."

"Liza hopes a child will bring some balance into her life," revealed an insider. "Liza believes she will be able to complete the adoption procedure as soon as January. She's thrilled about the adoption. Not only does she expect the child will save her marriage, she knows that it will keep love in her life. Liza knows that many of her friends have successfully managed career and family. That is what she wants for herself."

In support of all children, Liza appeared at a benefit for Denise Rich's G & P Charitable Foundation for Cancer Research. The party was held under a huge white marquee at Rich's house in The Hamptons on Sunday, September 1. Liza sang "I Can't Give You Anything But Love" — replacing the word "baby" with "David" — and called David onto the stage, where she was more affectionate than ever.

Liza would also be performing in "Liza's Christmas Spectacular" on December 5 and 6 at the Town Hall in New York. "Liza's Back!" the CD recorded at the Beacon Theater by record czar Clive Davis for J Records, was released October 29.

Davis held a "listening party" that month at the Equitable Building for Liza's long-awaited new CD. Invitations promised a "special appearance" by Liza herself. Davis came out and said, "We all know about Liza's battles with her knees and her arthritis and her alcoholism, but after you hear this album, you are going to realize that Liza is back and bigger and better than ever." He promised that the new album would rank with some of the greatest live recordings of all time.

At that point, many in the audience expected Liza, but all Davis did was play some cuts from the album. Forty-five minutes went by, and still, no Liza. Davis wrapped it up, saying, "Thank you all for coming, and now, ladies and gentlemen, I give you Liza Minnelli!"

A fragile-looking Liza emerged wearing a fur coat and miniskirt.

"Her face was white and she looked like a deer caught in the headlights," said one observer. Liza talked about meeting the Queen Mother while she was in London and singing "I'll Be Seeing You," a cappella in her honor.

"Clive asked me if I would sing it here this evening," she said, "But I could never match that performance, so we're going to listen to it on tape!"

They played the CD cut of "I'll Be Seeing You" while Liza stood clinging to Davis, her hand on her heart, eyes raised. Someone shouted, "For Chrissake, Liza, sing something!" but Liza just stood silently listening to herself.

At a September cancer benefit, Liza made the dramatic announcement that she was battling the disease. "I had a small spot of cancer removed from below my right eye," she told a stunned crowd gathered at Denise Rich's Long Island home. "You have to cry," she added. "Crying gets it out. I've been crying for the last few days."

Liza was also finding relief in clearing out old memories. A lifelong hoarder, she began cleaning house by auctioning off a huge chunk of her belongings at the end of October. Among the 1,000 items she was offering for sale was a Donna Karan gown she wore to the Academy Awards and a costume from "Rent-a-Cop." Liza was offering it in seven lots through a joint venture with Sotheby's and a web site called Gottahaveit.com.

"Since she and David Gest got married and have it in their heads to adopt a child, they decided it was time to give everything back to the fans," announced Robert Schagrin, president of Gotta Have It Auctions. Gest isn't getting rid of much of his own stuff, though. Schagrin said Gest had only thrown in a few items, including the first-ever best actress Oscar, presented to Janet Gaynor in 1929. Schagrin expected the loot to fetch at least $1 million. The least expensive item? You could probably get a piece of the costume jewelry for about $80.

On September 26, it was reported that David had sold his West Side bachelor pad for $3.9 million, almost twice what he paid for it. "We'll all miss him very much," chuckled one neighbor in the high-rise whose residents included Liam Neeson, Howard Stern and Regis Philbin.

The next day, the honeymooners called Liz Smith from Hawaii to protest newspaper reports they were battling. "This is absolute paradise, we have never been happier," Liza assured the columnist. She was down to 108 pounds and they would be returning to New York for a big party at the Equitable Center, where Clive Davis had unveiled the new J Records CD "Liza's Back!" This was her first album in more than two years, and Clive wanted to make it as big as "Judy Garland Live at Carnegie Hall."

In addition to everything else, David and Liza had been busy recording radio and television commercials for a new reality TV show, "Liza and David," which had been planned by VH1. The series was scheduled to begin Nov. 3, 2002, and the network also planned to air a half-hour special titled "Liza and David: The Wedding." Producer David Gest had promised it would include first-time footage — Natalie Cole singing "Unforgettable" — and glimpses of the 58 performers who did their stuff at the reception.

Gest was anxious to make it clear that their reality TV show was not "The Osbournes" or the "Anna

Nicole Show." He told Liz Smith that theirs would showcase their chemistry and musical guests from all over the world. Said Gest, "Not just in our apartment, but in Nashville, London, Africa and Monte Carlo."

By late October, there were rumors that the show was in trouble. "It is a nightmare," one source revealed. "VH1 was supposed to premiere the show in November. They have to try and do promotions and television specials on other shows for it, but Liza and David have yet to film even one segment of their program. Liza was intent on rehearsing. I guess she has no idea what reality TV means."

The show was postponed to December 8, then early January, and then it was suddenly canceled.

After shooting 60 hours of their lives — including a star-studded dinner party that turned into a fiasco — VH1 pulled the plug and launched a vicious public assault on David and Liza, claiming that they were denied access to Liza. David, they claimed, had been a flamboyant, demanding diva.

VH1 sources said that David kept Liza locked in their apartment, forced the crew to take off their shoes, and even ordered a female crew member to stick her head in their oven to make sure it was clean.

David and Liza insisted they had bent over backward to accommodate VH1 and got treated like doormats for their trouble. A livid Liza charged that the show's producer got physical with David, the crew turned their apartment into a shambles and they were badgered and humiliated in front of their guests.

"I even let them follow me to my AA meeting," Liza explained. "When I got there, I had to tell them, 'The reality is that you can't come inside.' But we didn't hide anything. Listen, I came out of the womb and somebody slapped me on the ass and I've been in the public ever since. I've never even had the luxury of being able to hide anything!"

The couple said they graciously allowed their apartment to be turned into a makeshift TV studio but were left with damage to furniture, walls and the ceiling. There were dangerous electrical wires and cables running everywhere. Gest even produced a letter from their apartment building's management company stating that VH1 had damaged a roof and violated the New York City fire code by illegally storing TV equipment in stairwells.

Although the network praised Liza, they claimed Gest was impossible to work with and he repeatedly canceled production meetings and halted shooting. One source said that David "redefines the term 'control freak.' He was almost insane."

Liza has stood by her man and claimed that the miserable VH1 experience had left them more in love than ever. Relaxing in the living room of their luxurious Manhattan penthouse, Liza repeatedly kissed and hugged her husband to underscore their love during their interview.

"They wrote that you keep me home in chains," Liza teased her husband.

David laughed, "Yeah, when people came to the house — I unchained her."

Despite the turmoil, Liza was disappointed by the cancellation, because she had hoped that their reality show would inspire others. "I thought I could help somebody through humor and now my sobriety," revealed Liza. "I have two fake hips. I have all spare parts. And I dance and do flips. Somebody lying in a hospital bed would maybe watch this thing, maybe a kid, and would want to get up and dance — and would know they could do it because I did it. That's what my husband and I both wanted."

Gest ripped into reports accusing him of odd or abusive behavior.

"They said that I made the crew wear 'surgical booties' to put up tracks of lights on the ceiling. They had to drill through reinforced concrete. What a mess it made on the marble floors! We just had the place renovated. All I did was ask a guy who was working to wear shoe covers, the kind painters wear. You would, too, if it was your house."

David also dismissed the story that he had ordered a female crew member to stick her head in the oven. "First of all, the oven has racks."

Gest went on: "I told one cameraman at least fifteen times to be careful around a particular Art Deco cabinet in the dining room. Of course, at the end of the night he managed to chip the glass. VH1 shot more than sixty hours — and they claim they don't have anything worth showing. They have Liza singing to kids at Sylvia's famous soul food restaurant in Harlem. They have us at Starbucks. They have Liza at her dance class and in central Park. They have me shopping at a food market, shopping for rugs and buying antiques and clothing."

Each episode of the show was to conclude with a star-studded dinner party at Liza's apartment. But the bitterness exploded into open warfare during the October 21 filming of the first dinner, attended by 60 guests.

"[Executive producer] Rob Weiss was very, very rude," bristled Gest. "I have never seen behavior like that, even from a child!"

Gest had invited Ray Charles, Luther Vandross, Ashford & Simpson and Deborah Cox to the bash and had them all rehearse before guests started arriving around 7 p.m.

"We didn't expect Sandra Bernhard, one of our guests, to ask to sing," said Gest, "But she did, and we welcomed her performance."

VH1 had asked singer Michelle Branch to attend, and David had invited Kelly Rowland of Destiny's Child. David recalls, "I did ask Kelly if she wanted to sing. She said not this time, but she would do so on a future episode. Kelly told ABC legal correspondent Cynthia McFadden, one of our guests, that she had been on the road and was too tired."

Liza added, "Before the performances, I asked Michelle if she wanted to sing. She told me, 'No, I came as a guest, but I'd love to come back another time.'"

VH1 executives had expected both Michelle and Kelly to sing on the first show.

David said that producer Weiss became agitated while Liza sang, "Maybe This Time" — and his anger exploded during her next number, "And the World Goes 'Round," a song dedicated to David.

"Weiss is screaming in my ear: 'You gotta put Kelly and Michelle on, and if you don't, your show is canceled!'" David recalled.

"He then said that the other artists who had performed earlier 'meant nothing' to him. He insulted Ray Charles, who is 72, and an icon and a legend. If you don't want to put on a television performance of Ray and Liza singing 'Georgia' together, you must be un-America!"

What outraged David the most was the way the VH1 producer treated Liza. "The most humiliating thing you can do to a performer, he did to Liza," said David. "She saw a man come up to me when she was singing two feet away and begin jabbing and poking me and making demands with his cell phone ringing! His actions made Liza worried and nervous. One guest told me that had Weiss done that to his wife while she was singing he would have punched him. I managed to restrain myself, but it was hard."

Liza confirmed David's account of the incident, right down to the jabbing and poking.

"Here I was, doing my job," she explained. "The film cameras were rolling. I was trying to do the best I could. Nothing like that has ever happened to me before — not even all those years performing in concert halls around the world."

As a final word on the entire fiasco, Liza herself has always said that, "Reality is something you rise above."

Once again, she achieved that goal.

Nowadays, David and Liza are focusing on something much more important than the canceled program — adopting their daughter.

"I'm looking forward to it so much," beamed Liza. "I honestly don't think it was time for a child in my life until I met David. God makes things happen for a reason — I believe that. The marriage is way beyond what I thought it would be. I married a very strong, wonderful man."

Concluded David: "We're more in love now than

the day we met. It's been almost nine months since our wedding. We beat the odds. Everybody was saying a week. I will do anything for my wife. If there was a bullet, I'd step in front of it. It's the greatest marriage."

Some things about Liza Minnelli will never change. She has always loved reading about other people's pasts. Most of the movie projects she's tried to get going have been biographies of others. But she did not like reading about her own past.

"The past is finished for me," she once said. "I lived it. So I can't think why it should be so interesting."

Once, Liza accused her mother of being full of self-pity. Judy turned to her, smiling, and said, "Don't you understand? Sympathy is my business!"

"That was what I learned from Mama," said Liza, her face beaming. "Survival."

☆☆☆☆☆☆☆☆☆☆☆☆☆☆☆☆☆☆☆☆
☆　　　　**ACKNOWLEDGMENTS**　　　　☆
☆☆☆☆☆☆☆☆☆☆☆☆☆☆☆☆☆☆☆☆

This book exists because of the blazing talent of one Liza May Minnelli, and I salute her!

I have relied to a great extent on many caring friends of Liza who preferred to stay anonymous. I thank them all.

Special gratitude goes to the investigative reporters of the National Enquirer, the Star and the Globe, who continue to keep it real.

I am thankful for the resources of the New York Public Library for The Performing Arts, and the endless patience and unfailing good humor of the library staff.

I also wish to thank Patricia Towle for encouraging me to take on this project.

Finally, thanks to Michael Clark for his unwavering support.

Sarah Gallick, January 2003